IGNITE YOUR *Truth*

SET YOUR SOUL ON FIRE

Christie Hayden

Difference Press

McLean, Virginia, USA

Copyright © Christie Hayden, 2018

All rights reserved. No part of this book may be reproduced in any form without permission in writing from the author. Reviewers may quote brief passages in reviews.

Published 2018

ISBN: 978-1-68309-006-9

DISCLAIMER

No part of this publication may be reproduced or transmitted in any form or by any means, mechanical or electronic, including photocopying or recording, or by any information storage and retrieval system, or transmitted by email without permission in writing from the author.

Neither the author nor the publisher assumes any responsibility for errors, omissions, or contrary interpretations of the subject matter herein. Any perceived slight of any individual or organization is purely unintentional.

Brand and product names are trademarks or registered trademarks of their respective owners.

Cover Design: Jennifer Stimson

Editing: Anna Paradox

Author's photo courtesy of Joshua Hayden

Dedication

For my amazing husband, and two beautiful children who inspire, motivate, and ground me every single day. I would not ever have made it to the point I am at now if it wasn't for the love, support, and beautiful memories we've shared.

"Forever thine, forever mine, forever us."

– Beethoven

TABLE OF CONTENTS

INTRODUCTION vii

Chapter One WHY AM I HERE? 21
"Because My Lizard Said So…"

Chapter Two CLIMBING THE WALLS 31
"Oh My. We Aren't in Kentucky Anymore"

Chapter Three THE JOURNEY AHEAD 45
"Pretty-Girl Bawz On"

Chapter Four SHEDDING THE SHITAKES 49
"Let It Go, Let It Go"

Chapter Five I CAN SEE CLEARLY NOW 57
"Bigger, Brighter, Bolder"

Chapter Six EVERYTHING STARTS WITH YOU 69
"Ignite the Flame"

Chapter Seven UNLEASH THE MAGIC WITHIN YOU 79
"Magical as Fluff"

Chapter Eight COLOR OUTSIDE THE LINES 89
"Outside of the Box Thinking"

Chapter Nine   FEEL THE FEAR AND DO IT ANYWAY   97
"Sound the Alarms"

Chapter Ten   CREATING A LINE IN THE SAND   105
"Did Someone Order Boundaries?"

Chapter Eleven   FACE THE WOMAN IN THE MIRROR   109
"Smexy and I Know It"

Chapter Twelve   CHALLENGES   115
"Cue the Lights"

CONCLUSION   121
"No Turning Back Now"

FURTHER READING   124

ACKNOWLEDGMENTS   125

ABOUT THE AUTHOR   127

ABOUT DIFFERENCE PRESS   128

OTHER BOOKS BY DIFFERENCE PRESS   130

THANK YOU   131

INTRODUCTION

Once upon a time, I thought quotes like this "Be fearless in the pursuit of what sets your soul on fire," were nothing more than bull shitake. I used to believe we had no say in how our lives would turn out or evolve. I felt only rich snobs would even create these sayings, and who the heck really understood what they were even talking about? What the fluff is woo-woo? I thought it was another term to describe what my grandmother used to call a woman's coin purse (and I'm talking about the one in your pants). Least to say I was totally clueless.... Keep in mind, at the time I was in a very dark, damp, lonely fluffing place. There was so much I desperately needed to change in my life, and I felt immense anger for anything religious or spiritual due to my glorious upbringing ... where religion was a forced meal. However, had I been able to see past my nose, and the current cesspool I was comfortable in, I might have awakened much, much sooner.

My journey is not one for the faint of heart, but it's a very important place to start because I know you will be able to relate.

Growing up in poverty, in the boondocks of "Bible Belt" Kentucky – where faith was all that anyone ever had to talk about – was pretty fluffin' tough for a young girl who had nothing. It seemed praying to Jesus was always the answer, and no matter how many times I prayed, all I ever heard was crickets' chirp. As a young girl, I remember being forced on the weekly church van by my fabulous mother.... Her excuse was, "You have to go to church because I need a fluffin' break." Boy, did it strike a chord within me. I didn't ever enjoy going to church listening to the manmade horse crap, and being told we were all children of God. Well if God is so real then why the heck am I suffering like I am? Why would he ever condone these situations? For example, I remember being so hungry right before the church bus would arrive that I'd open a can of hominy and eat it. Yep, right out of the can because we didn't have gas for the stove, and I'm sure you guessed it ... what was a microwave? Upon arriving to church, we were always the first kids in line for the cookies. I mean, I would think it was pretty obvious to the outside world that we were fluffing hungry, and that praying wasn't working – at least for me. I spent countless nights praying, crying, and wishing my life would end with some miraculous alien disappearance because it was so fluffin' painful. As many of you can imagine, there were times as a child I went without food, clothing, heat, hot water, a bath, soap, or just the bare necessities because my mom worked all the time, but was only making a servant's wage at $5.25 an hour. Seriously. It was just enough for rent, her carton of cigarettes, and a few cans of potted meat.

As the oldest of five, I was awarded the amazing job title of babysitter, mother, housekeeper, and tutor, and I taught myself how to cook, how to creatively mix shtuff together and make it taste descent. I also learned how to sew, crochet, and when all else failed, use duct tape. I have always been that nurturing, mothering, loving, responsible, and an old soul.... And the question I pondered the most is: Why in the heck would so-called God put me on this Earth to suffer the way I have? I couldn't understand it ... for the longest time I stayed stuck right there, even though *deep* down I knew I was meant for so much more. I've always felt I had a higher calling, a bigger purpose, a mission on the planet, and my grandma used to tell me that I carried the weight of the world on my shoulders.... Boy was she right.

Fast forward a few years, and I got my first job as a waitress at a little joint called "Steak-n-Shake." Dang I was happy. Finally, I was out of the house, I could catch my breath, and I actually even bought my first ever pair of brand-spankin' new name-brand sneakers. I know – quite small in the realm of things – but *dang* it felt amazing. I felt like I was on top of the world, as long as I didn't have to go home. Going home ... I faced more than many of you bargained for by purchasing this book, but I'll briefly discuss it. I faced verbal, sexual, physical, and mental abuse in every aspect of the words. I was made to feel like I was a powerless victim, worthless, ugly, disappointing, as I was often told I would never amount to anything. For example, on more than one occasion, when getting my bowl of whatever the fluff we were eating that night, my step-monster would trip me and tell me to eat my food off the floor like the dog that I was. You see, I wasn't his child, and he'd made sure I was super aware of that from the moment he stepped into my life at the age of three. Keep in mind, that since we were poor we only had five chairs, and there were six of us, so of course I was the one chosen to eat off the floor – but to be honest, I always preferred that if anyone was going to face mistreatment, that it was indeed me.

As you may have already discovered, I have always been the "black sheep" of the family, and for the longest time it made me cower inside ... afraid to be who I really was, and wishing to be everything I wasn't. I wanted so badly to fit in, to look like my siblings ... because just maybe if I was tall, had blonde hair, blue eyes, and a pretty smile then I'd be loved too. Let's just say many of you know this was never the case, but deep down inside I yearned for it ... for love. Any love, any kind, just to matter. Could someone please show me they cared.... That I mattered?

Well, without further ado, let's talk about another skelly in the old closet. At a very young age, I started being sexually assaulted, and raped by the one person who I thought loved me, and often showered me with gifts ... my grandfather. This carried on for a few years before the secret was revealed ... while my grandfather was on his deathbed, let's just say. I was still a young child and worried deeply about getting him into trouble, not to mention there was always that deep scary verbal threat that if I told anyone about what was going on I'd be sorry. Deep inside, in an eerie, sick, gross-arse way, I knew him to be the only person who actually loved me. Needless to say, my mother asked me if I'd ever been touched by my grandfather, and my face lit up like an eccentric Christmas tree... *Bingo!* (dead giveaway). Bawling, I held on to my mother's leg, and begged her to not get him in trouble.... Needless to say, my mother decided to confront him on his deathbed, and half a day later, my grandfather passed away. I bet you can guess what happened next.... Yep! She came home, and told me she had confronted him (I was nine or ten at the time), and that he had passed away. So guess who added that guilt to their already overflowing plate? That's right. Me.

I wish I could tell you that this was all absolutely a bull-crap fictional story, as many of you may be shocked, but this is just the very beginning piece of my amazing journey. Why am I sharing? I want to be 100 percent as transparent, honest, and forthcoming as I can ... to show you that if one broke-as-fluff, mentally, physically, emotionally unstable being can change their life around in an instant, then so can you. Keep in mind, I was overcoming a fluff-ton of challenging obstacles in order to be the beautiful light I am today; however, in the moment... it abso-fluffing-lutely sucked, and while going through most of it, I felt like a hopeless victim in every sense of the words.

In high school, I had one more significantly beautiful trauma occur that, little did I know, would forever change my life. I hit rock bottom in a way I hope no one else ever does. Yep. I had finally had enough of the abuse, the bull crap, and decided it was finally time to stand up for myself to the step-monster. This time, I had my pretty-girl "bawz" on, and felt ten feet tall. I was ready! He slapped me across the face for verbally holding my ground, and in return, I pretty much punched him full force in the arm.

His retaliation was to raise his nasty ol' wrinkly hand, and slap me two more times across my face ... before my mom finally came in and broke it up. My cheeks were swollen, red, and it looked as though I'd just been in a fight with a row boat paddle. Instead of comforting me, instead of loving me, instead of asking if I was okay... she yelled at me, grounded me, and told me to go to fluffing school. As I left tears welled up in my eyes. I knew this time that standing up for myself was different. I felt it. Upon coming home from school later that day, I realized there was a black plastic garbage bag sitting next to the front door, and I bet you could guess what was in it ... my stuff. There it was, a bag – not even filled to the brim – with every single thing I owned ... one black plastic garbage bag that held the contents of my whole fluffing life. Was this all I would ever have, would ever be, and was this what would define the rest of my life? In this moment, I felt absolutely horrible, victimized, helpless, and as though my whole life just came crashing to the ground. After staring at the black satchel, and pondering, my mom came out to make sure I was aware that I was to take my black garbage bag and get the fluff off the porch, out of the house, out of their life.... Officially, I was terrified, saddened, bawling, my eyes were so swollen, my tummy so hungry as I never had school lunch money, and we didn't qualify for free lunches. All I could repeat is I am a homeless high school senior with nowhere to go. What would I do? I got a brave idea to call my aunt who had once pretended to care about me, the abuse, etc. However, since then, she'd sided with my mom (she was her best friend, after all). Well, to no great surprise she told me I couldn't stay with her because she didn't want to betray my mom. I made call after call to a lot of my so-called family ... but I received the same response: no room, no way, no answer. As I hugged my siblings (a.k.a. my kids) goodbye, I broke down in tears, grabbed my bag full of shitake, and walked down the sidewalk. I had nowhere to go, no one to speak with, no way of communicating ... what was I going to do? I walked to school and noticed there was still someone in the office. They allowed me to call a friend from the office phone to ask for a ride.

My beautiful friend took me home with her, and said I could stay over for a few days. Thankfully, two days later, my uncle, who lived an hour away, called me and said I could stay with him. I was so grateful, my eyes welled up with tears. I would knowingly have a safe place to lay my head, and I was terrified as well because I would be an hour away from everything I'd ever known even though it hadn't ever really been that much. Of course, I had no car, no money, and a trash bag full of used clothing to my name. It would be one heckuva struggle with school, but I knew it was for the best. Every single morning, I'd wake up at 5 a.m. to get ready for school, in order to catch a ride with my uncle (who worked near my school) and sit at school for two hours before the first-class bell rang. After school, I'd have to wait for my uncle to take that hour-long haul back, eat, and then go to bed. Not once during the whole time there did my mom ever call me. I was heart-broken. I bawled daily. I missed my siblings so much. I felt so fluffing lonely, misplaced, and depressed. So much so, that I kept channeling that song, "There Is a Stranger in My House."

I ended up graduating with honors from high school, and the night of my graduation, my mom finally made her first call to my uncle – inquiring on whether I was still going to school, and if I was actually going to graduate tonight. I literally felt my heart crumble into pieces on the floor, and tears rushed down my face like a dam's walls imploding. Why would she doubt my intelligence? The only thing my mom had ever complimented me for is how dang smart I am. She would brag to everyone she knew about my intelligence, and even carried my report card around in her purse to show off. It was the only real thing I ever felt she was proud of me for.

In spite of everything, and everyone else's doubt, I graduated. I was so freakin' proud of myself because in the face of all the obstacles and adversity, I realized just how fluffing resilient I truly was. For the first time in my whole life, I knew I could do anything I could set my mind to, and that this was only the very beginning.

This beautiful realization allowed me to forever change my mindset. I ended up buying my first car, I put myself through college, stood on my own two fluffin' feet, *but* I still felt like the biggest failure deep inside. I still felt so dang unworthy, unloved, and abandoned ... the one relationship I had craved my entire human life was the one with my mother, and it was so very broken.

Keep in mind, my father was never in the picture. He was a mere figment of my imagination, and nothing more than a sperm-donor. I never even got an opportunity to meet him, which stung for a long time. I had so many questions, but on my eighteenth birthday I finally got the opportunity to call him, and as soon as I said my name ... he knew who I was, and told me to never call him again. He claimed I was an embarrassment to his life as he's a 90-year-old dirty fluffing sleaze of a man who had two lives, and sadly passed away last year in December.

So, the only parental connection I ever had was with my mom. Which is probably part of the reason I yearned so deeply for her unconditional love, her affection, attention, and I spent thirty years jumping through hoops, people-pleasing, giving her every last fluffing penny to my name to get it.... There was not anything I wouldn't do for her (cue Bryan Adams). *Insanity* at its finest.

Last year, I finally decided "enough was enough," and it was time to be "all in' on myself. It was time to put myself first, and that literally meant finally severing the tie to my mother ... which terrified the shitakes out of me. However, after reliving the same lesson 254 times, even the most unaware being starts to notice the pattern. The epiphany finally came out of left field ... woman, it was the big one: I realized that I could not fix her, I could not save her, nor could I make her change. I could not force it – even though I desired to on such a deep level. This realization cut me to my core because it was as if I were a child giving up hope that Santa Claus was real.... In the passing moments, I started to come to terms with the fact that it's okay to have all the hope in the world for her, but I can only lead her to the water ... it's on her to drink. Talk about painful ... that was the *most* painful, heart-wrenching realization to date: Realizing I couldn't save her. I couldn't rescue her from her own fluffing crazed illusionary prison.

That being said, it became even more obvious that it was finally time to cut the ethereal cord. I did this by allowing myself to see that she had indeed already completed her mission for me in this life. Thus, I am grateful for her giving me life, and teaching me what I did not ever want, acquire, or need in my own life. I wish her well in love and light. I do indeed still allow communication as I have two beautifully new babies, *but* since cutting that cord ... I have no expectation, and boundaries are most definitely in place, as I refuse to be pulled back down that rabbit hole into the dark winding abyss.

The moral of the journey is that once you choose to put yourself first – once you choose to be "all in" bawz deep on you – that's when all of the magic truly starts to happen. That is when you start to see life in a bigger, more beautiful way. This is also when your life starts to really unfold, right before your very eyes. Thus, I'm assuming if you're reading this ... then you too are acknowledging you feel called to a higher purpose, and some shitake in your life isn't as amazing as it might look exteriorly either. From one mask wearer to another, I want you to know that, the moment you decide to drink from the water, your life will change. Once you set that intention and put yourself first, the switch flips, and the realm of possibility opens. The beautiful news is that in order to unleash the magic within you, and be a bad-arse, fearless warrior, all you have to do is make one teensy shift. <u>Go from wanting to change your life, to deciding to make shitake happen.</u> Keep in mind, you'll probably have to do things you have never dreamed of, might even be embarrassed to be caught doing them, but fluff – to have the freedom, flexibility, and financial abundance you dream about ... isn't it worth it?

Keep in mind, this beautiful book is going to help guide you, to help you make the decision to be "all in, bawz deep on you." It's also going to walk you through the process of how to "make shitakes happen," and to "love the shitakes out of yourself." It's going to teach you some brand-spankin" new techniques and tricks to creating the life you desire, as well as the importance of owning your own shitakes. *But* it's also going to have you believing in shitakes that you cannot readily see with the naked eye, and you'll be pushing past your fears... living on the edge of your seat, failing forward. Keep in mind, it's all part of that beautifully vibrant bigger picture, the gorgeous process to making your dreams a reality. Throughout the process, you'll be "shedding the shitake" that's kept you chasing your tail, you'll be punching pillows, stomping mud holes in a paper or two's arse, and patting yourself on the back every step of the way. Odd enough? Well the cold-hard truth is the beautiful life you have envisioned ... the one you've already dreamed up in your mind's eye ... that life depends on the process.

You've probably heard of people having *huge* fluffin' breakthroughs where the shitake has hit the fan, and they rose like the phoenix from the ashes ... well that's exactly what happens. We strip you naked, and only put the items back on that are aligned with your highest purpose, intention, and are of your highest fluffing good.

Keep in mind, my main goal at first was launching my successful entrepreneurial business and making a difference in the world one person at a time. Little did I realize that it was sooo much more ... so much more, and that the money would just come with ease and flow. It still just shows up. For example, I had a $500 check last week just magically appear in my mailbox – no shitakes! When you are in alignment, believing, trusting, and knowing that the Universe has your back, and all you have to do is show up and be you ... that's where all your dreams come true.

Thus, in order to get you where you desire to be, you have to do things you've never done before. Therefore, I am going to present some amazing new ways, ideas, and processes to you throughout the journey of this book, and I am hopeful you'll stay open-minded and roll right along with me. As you'll see, they are backed by proven results not only for me, but my clients. In laymen's terms that means "they fluffing work." I'm not one to just blow smoke up your arse, but in order to get where you want to go, you've got to be willing to dig in, and be willing to change.

Your message needs to be heard, and I am hoping by purchasing this book, you are ready to take the steps necessary to "make shitakes happen." The world needs more compassionate, caring, intellectual, understanding, and wealthy individuals to really step up and to make a difference in the world. I always live by this quote by Gandhi, as it's a favorite *"Be the change you wish to see in the world."*

We need those who are ready to share love, messages, their fluffing secrets to success with the world without worrying about money ... because here's the thing you're going to see. Once you show up of service in your highest self, the money comes all on its own. Remember, we live in a world of limitless possibilities, and there is indeed more than enough for every single one of us, all you have to do is choose to believe.... After all, what do you really have to lose?

Now's the time to take a deep breath, tell yourself you've got this, grab your warrior suit, and dive in with an open mind. You can choose to read this book and say "what a load of shitakes," or you can open that beautifully creative mind of yours, and try this shitake on for size. You'll see that holy shitakes ... it worked. Then guess what? You'll rinse, repeat, and test it again, and *bam*, you slay. One day, you'll wake up and realize you did it. You have completely broke free of the confinements within the box, you are fluffing living your dream, and bam, that's when you'll feel the most appreciative and grateful you ever have (minus having babies because, just being honest, for me that was just absolutely miraculous). So, with that being said, let's get this beautiful journey started.

Chapter One

WHY AM I HERE?

"What got you here, won't get you there."
– James Wedmore

"Because My Lizard Said So…"

Six months ago, I was in my creative zone teaching a virtual course on empathy, self-confidence, and the importance of trusting yourself, when all of a sudden, mid-lesson I hear a voice on the loud speaker say "You are a hypocrite." As I looked around to see if I were nutty butters, or one screw shy of being condemned … it hit me like a ton of bricks landing on my chest … Holy shitakes… they found me out… I'm a phony, a fake, not worthy, a fluffing loser with a capital L, and nope I don't believe half the shitake I'm teaching. How in the heck can I guide or lead this fabulous student so dang effectively on how to be a top-performer, and not really believe most of the shitake I was spewing internally? I finished the class, as quickly as possible, avoiding the comment I heard over the loud speaker in my own head, and started pondering what this could all be....

Finally, after what seemed like hours, of rehearing that sarcastic, but nonetheless true voice that startled me mid-class ... I was able to calm my lizard, ease my mind, and slow the stream of thoughts.

It was in this golden moment of opportunity that I realized that even after all of the shitakes I had been through ... after all of the childhood and adolescent trauma, and all the work I thought I had done on myself to heal ... there it was again, right in my face, written in sharpie ... I still felt unworthy, unloved, and like a phony ... and instead of embracing it, owning it, or letting it go... I decided to run and hide for another month because the life I had created wasn't terrible – it just wasn't exactly what I desired. Exactly what I dreamed of, exactly what is my purpose, but how could it be when I continuously chose to allow fear to win. For auto-pilot to take over because I knew it was safe. I knew what to expect, and I didn't have to worry about failing, falling, or facing the uncomfiness of the shtuff still hiding in my invisi-closet that was filled to the brim. Instead I could continue wearing the "mask of many colors," and pretending to be fulfilled, happy, and in my lane.

What a pivotal moment in my journey, and my handy-dandy lizard definitely took it upon his self, to try and make me un-hear what I knew to be true ... Keep in mind, what I am or will be referring to as "our lizard," throughout the journey of this beautiful book, is none other than our fabulous "ego." Also known as our subconscious mind which is much like your "inner child" in that he holds on for dear life to the unfiltered information we claim to be our beliefs, as they came from other people such as mom, dad, siblings, family, friends, and instead of testing it, researching it, many of us just thought, "Well, they wouldn't lie, and it sounds true enough." Therefore, we've been packing this shitake around subconsciously like Santa with a bag over his shoulder.... When we attempt to go against the grain, our lizard comes out, stomping his feet, and freakin' the fluff out to get us back in that "safe zone." That safe zone is the box where we let him steer, be in control ... the box that holds the merry-go-round we like to consistently ride. "Get back in the box," he whispered, "as it's safe, you know the outcome, you know it's trusty, you know what to expect."

Is that really all that I want for my life? Is that all I aspire to do? Is that the life I want my kids to know, and to learn? Is that really all I have to offer? Is this my reality? My purpose? A fluffing box, with a lizard that likes to play in the kiddie pool, I've created for myself? "*Fluff that*," I shouted, fist closed. I decided it's time to leap, it's time to change ... *But* how?

Keep in mind, before we move forward into the understanding, the "what", we must first understand the "why."

Thus, with that being said, the subconscious mind (a.k.a. the lizard) holds the blueprint to our life, and often runs on the so-called beliefs we inherited from others as a child without question.

Most of the time we are running on "auto-pilot," and have no idea that these beliefs, or that the lizard, even exist.... He likes to keep it that way, as it keeps you small, safe, and in the sand box with all the other kids. It's not until we hit the wall face first, hit rock bottom, or start to ask questions that we discover ... fluff, there's something else in control.

Once our conscious mind finally gets on the same page and is made aware that a little fear-based lizard is trying to run the show...We finally start asking the quality questions that lead us to knowing safe is small. Small is not a "game-changer," and we are constantly playing by someone else's rules, regulations, and ideas. *Fluff that*! I'm a sacred rebel at heart, and I am positive, if you're reading this, you are too.

This is why you are still chasing your tail, why you stumble and fall. Why you feel stuck, fluffing unfulfilled ... it's because the lizard is running the show even though our conscious mind likes to put blinders on, pretending it is. For example, let's say you grew up with parents who worked 40-50 hours a week to make shitakes happen. Struggling financially but hustling so that you didn't have to do without. Let's say you overheard them constantly bicker about money, and how it doesn't grow on trees, there's never enough ... well what happens is your beautifully clever lizard takes it at face value, and *bam* you have your first subconscious limiting belief ... that money is bad, evil, scarce, and hard to get.

Now to show you how this works... as an adult consciously living, you are striving to make a shitake amount of money in abundance, and hustling ... working your arse off because you desire to be able to swim in your millions like Scrooge McDuck ... (Maybe not the last bit, but you get the big picture). However, because subconsciously you still believe money is scarce, hard to get, and evil, you will notice how every time you get ahead, you fall back three steps, or that it comes into your life with hustle, and it's so dang hard to hang on to.... What's happening is you are manifesting the belief that money is scarce, evil, hard to get, and it all has to do with that inherited belief system. *Yep!* Crazy shtuff, I know. Don't kill your lizard just yet, because I want you to keep in mind he means well, he really does... But he worries about you, and as soon as you step foot outside the "safe zone" you have created, he starts to think "If you do this you will lose something or someone you love, or harm will come to you, and *big* red flags, alerts, and sirens are a-wailing.'

Therefore, if you have subconscious limiting beliefs, and trust me – *we all do* – it's going to stop you right in your tracks and keep you from what you desire the most. Success, tons of money, or possibly even love. For example, let's say you grew up in a single mommy home... where you witnessed your dad abandon ship, and how much pain it caused your mom, as well as yourself. You observed mom dating men, who also just left, disappeared, wouldn't commit for the long-haul.... Subconsciously you are taking in this belief system that men don't like to stay, men are not loyal, not trustworthy, and they might hurt you. No, I know you didn't mean to, but this is exactly what happens. We learn from modelling, observation, and then good ol' word of mouth as children, and as studies have shown, we tend to learn the most at a very young age.

Keep in mind, we don't realize we are doing it. It's all under the radar, and we inherited beliefs for a reason. However, this is why when we hear that little voice – often referred to as your soul self, or highest self – say "no more," sometimes we keep doing it anyways ... it's simply because we aren't aligned, in tune with our soul, or our heart-center which is really what should be illuminating our path, and the ego says look, there's another one. Which creates a chaotic mess between the light and what we'll deem the shadow self. The light self is our heart-center, it's what illuminates, inspires, motivates, and allows us to stand out ... The shadow self of course is the lizard and remember, he's not bad at all. An analogy that I quite often hear is it's like driving with one foot on the gas, and one foot on the brake. You aren't going to get very far. The shadow self just wants to keep us safe – that's his primary job, and what we need is them both in balance like the yin-and-yang. Another example, that may ring a bell for you is: Dang, I need to lose 20 pounds, but you've seen the models on television who have lost weight, and now have eating disorders, or suffer from a subscription to the latest fad diet, plastic surgery, or weight-loss pill ... now your subconscious has planted the thought that losing weight may cause you harm, so I better protect myself and bubble up. Thus, one reason why you may be carrying extra weight.

Another example I want to discuss with you is "people pleasing." I bet you'll be able to resonate. Up until six months ago, I was too afraid to speak up, to use my voice, to be in conflict with another being, so I'd just bite my tongue, smile, and nod, or my favorite: walk away. It's that beautiful flight or fight theory, and my brain would always choose flight. Have you ever felt fearful of standing up for yourself, fearful of being in conflict because dang that means someone doesn't like me, I might be bullied, or maybe I won't fit in? I guarantee you have because many of us experience this at some point in our life.

Why in the heck do we think our opinions, our beliefs, our truths, our voices are any less worthy than someone else's? Well ... (hint, hint wink, wink) maybe because they were once silenced, taken from us, and we were told that girls are to be seen and not heard? Maybe you even saw your mother be silenced by your father, her father, or even her own mother, and you again learn from observation... taking it in to mean that our words, our voices, because we are females, do not matter. And then add all the crazy sexist arseholes of the world who make sly remarks like *a women's place is in the home, in the kitchen, make me a sandwich*, or some other asinine fluffing disrespectful, untrue injustice. Our lizard silently processes these Easter eggs as truths ... at face value. Maybe you even saw your mom or you were passed up for a hard-fluffing earned promotion to your worthless (in love and light) co-worker simply because he has a real scrotum... These would all tie to that throat chakra being blocked, and feeling as though your voice, your opinions, your ideas, and your beliefs are not worth hearing. Which is ab-so-lutely fluffing nutty butters. However, deep down I bet you felt a tug ... because you know it's true. As a woman, in America in the year 2018, we still have bull crap we deal with on the daily... just for being a woman, and it's pretty fluffing lame. However, like Oprah said, "Our time is up." This is the year of the divine feminine, and we are indeed going to rise up, and own our shitake.

Which brings me to our next topic.... Do you find yourself doubting every single thing you do, or hiding out at home? Yep, I mean being a home-body, hermit, having to wear ten gallons of face paint before you go out... Let me ask you, why do you feel called to do this? Is it because you are worried about what somebody else will say, think, feel, or how they will treat you? *Bingo!* Why does someone else's opinions, ideas, feelings, matter more than your own? Why in the heck do we put strangers' fluffing thoughts above our own? Have you noticed, you have to make sure you glance at the mirror, check your face paint, and outfit for flaws before you leave your house? Do you notice that you are constantly doubting which color shoes to wear today, what someone might say about this hat (even though you secretly love it)? These are all people pleasing, self-doubt ways, and they stem from one of the inherited beliefs we spoke about of not feeling worthy, enough, ugly, overweight, or etc....

This could be from seeing how aesthetically unattractive people are treated by society and adapting that belief about yourself. Remember, we are always our toughest critic, and maybe being ten pounds overweight makes you feel like you are "Free Willy," ready for take-off... or that could just be your lizard. These thoughts don't just disappear, and I am sure you notice they come up often. Hint: Probably every single day, when you see yourself naked in the shower, look in the mirror to put on your war paint, or see some super skinny girl on the boob tube.

All they are is doubt. A seed of doubt that was planted long ago via observation, or language with someone you once looked up to as a role model, or deeply trusted … usually it's your parents, or those super-duper close to you. For example, seeing a chubby girl who wears no makeup at school being picked on: *trigger, trigger, trigger alert*, and bam now you always make sure you are working out, thin, hiding any extra weight, and of course, you are now wearing face paint before you ever leave your house. Of course, you are wearing spanx to suck in that extra chub-a-wubba. Of course, you are hiding out when you have a cold sore, a black eye, or feel extra bloated… you don't ever want to have to feel like you saw that chubby girl being treated. Make sense?

Mind you, it's important to remember that you cannot have one side without the other, but you will soon discover that the key to it all is awareness.

Therefore, until you are aware of what is really going on, and able to understand it, you'll keep working on the surface level, trying to fix it or change the aesthetics, instead of pulling the weed out by the roots. Which is why you see so many beautiful human beings, hustling for their dreams, getting a bit of success, and then landing right on their face. It's because there is still some deeply-seeded bull crap that we are telling ourselves underneath the surface.

Not buying it yet? Well, let's start with what I like to call a little warm-up… Ask yourself this, "Are you making as much money as you are capable of making?" Do you notice that as you make money, it leaves you quickly, or that your salary is capped off at a certain number that you are finding almost dang near impossible to rise above? If so, let's ask you this, what are your parents' beliefs about money, and how was money referred to in the household? Fill in this blank: When I think about money, the first thing that pops into my head is _____. (Do it for as many words that pop up, jot it down, look over it, and notice how it feels).

Keep in mind, this is just a warm-up to making you aware of how the subconscious and conscious mind work, as well as how manifestation works because remember, if we think money doesn't grow on trees ... that's a scarcity mind-set, and money will be scarcely provided to us. As we continue on in this beautiful book, you will gain the skill set, tools for your brand-spankin' new bag that will allow you to remove these beliefs by the root and replace them with truth and love. This is not only going to up your manifestation game, but up level your fluffing life.

Chapter Two

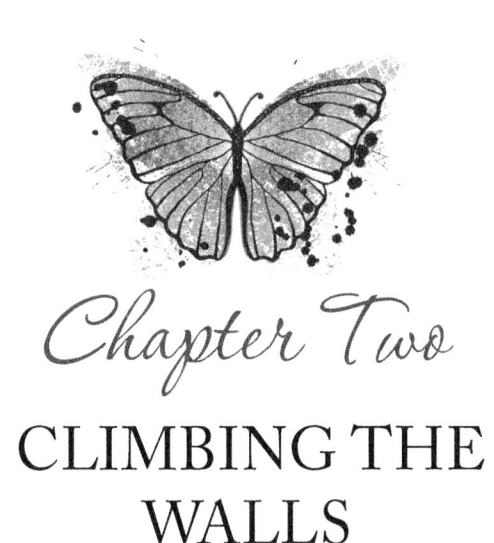

CLIMBING THE WALLS

"What you think, you become."

– Buddha

"Oh My. We Aren't in Kentucky Anymore"

After discovering that there was definitely some deep-rooted shitake I was still holding onto that no longer served me ... I realized I really have a choice to make I can either: a) Shove it in my invisi-closet, or b) Suit up in my smexy warrior suit and put my pretty bawz on because it's time to step into the unknown. This would include "shedding the shitake" that no longer serves my highest self, as well as being willing to live on the edge of my seat. Being present in my own dang life and making decisions and taking action instead of being on "auto-pilot."

The first step in the whole process was really to take a deep breath or three in through my mouth and exhale out through my nose. I then started with a peaceful guided meditation. Yep. Meditation is so dang important to help calm the lizard, to get grounded, centered, and to connect to your highest self. Meditations are everywhere nowadays, so you can find one on almost every YouTube channel. The most important key is to pick the one that musically resonates with you.

Once I completed my meditation, and found myself feeling more focused, clearer, and full of momentum, I knew it was time to really dive deep, face first, into what I was really holding onto, and why. Thus, I started by asking myself a simple question, "What was I really holding onto that was standing in the way of everything I desired?" I sat with the question allowing my body to respond, and really discovering the depths of each word... of course my body reacted. I felt a sharp pain in my chest, and a discomfort in my gut, and a few moments later, it came right on out. The unworthiness around my mom, the unconditional love I desired from my mom, the feeling that I was hideous because my mom told me I wasn't pretty like my sister, and that I am so dang fat because again, my mom continued to tell me this, every chance she got. At the core of who I was, I believed my mom. Even though I didn't realize it –I thought I loved myself, I thought I had released a lot of shitake around feeling unworthy, released the love I sought after, and released my fear of failure (because of course I was never going to amount to anything according to my family) – instead I had developed people-pleasing ways, and wore a "mask of many colors."

Sobbing, snotty booger tears began to run down my face, and I then realized – fluff me... I've been letting these untrue-arse thoughts run my life. They have been leading my life, and having me live in fear, in a box, as a fluffing cookie-cutter version of myself.

Awareness is the key to everything. Once your eyes are open, you cannot un-see. I knew this was it, the big enchilada that's been standing in my way for so dang long. Thus, what I decided to do was grab a pen and paper. Yep. I started writing down everything that I felt, and that I knew was standing in my way – allowing myself to journal like I never had before. I feel so dang unworthy because my mother despised me and told me I'd never amount to anything. She showed me that I was worthless on many accounts, and how my dad not being there was 100 percent on me. My mother made me feel disgusting about being sexually abused as a child by stating I was nasty and knew better. She continued to tell me how sick, twisted, and fluffed up my mind was. Keep in mind, as I write all of these painstakingly horrible things down, I'm BAWLING, releasing... allowing myself to feel the feels. Allowing myself to go there, to really release the power it's had over my life, by processing it before I bid it ado. The next topic I wrote down was feeling ugly and fat because I wasn't a blonde, blue-eyed, American, apple-pie kind of girl like my siblings. They all had beautiful blonde hair, and some shade of blue eyes ... not me. I was referred to as the "ugly duckling," Pinocchio, and Bucky the beaver simply because I wasn't pretty enough or important enough for braces. Bawling, releasing, and I continued the painstakingly horrible list.

When I finally wrote down every foul fluffing thing I had held on to for so long, it included being bullied in school for being poor, or having tattered clothing, as well as being picked on for always being the new girl, and never having haircuts or school supplies. I mean, I went in deep because these were things I subconsciously packed on to my back to carry around as my own version of the cross. I even wrote down the time my so-called best friend told me I'd never go to college. No idea why she said that then, but apparently it fluffed with me, and boy did I prove her arse wrong. "Bye, Felicia." My point here is this list should be two miles long, 400 tears deep, and you'll have to shed it more than once … promise I did. So, don't get hung up on the number of times or amount of shitake you're packing… Size really does not matter. Therefore, carry forward with caution if you are not ready, but then again, if you are not ready, you'll find a way to resist… to make excuses to not let it happen.

The next step, after allowing myself to journal every single word, and feel the feels was to write or say aloud three ways I knew that the statements I'd written down were not true. I started with I am not ugly, I am beautiful. I am not unworthy, I am worth every fluffing penny. I am not like my mother because I love unconditionally, I care deeply, and I am soo dang empathetically understanding. I am enough because I have always been, and I have always made shitake happen, I have always pushed through, and I love who I am.

"How do I know I'm not ugly?" my lizard spits at me.... Well I know I am not ugly because I was a model, and because I met the man of my dreams, and I have received so many dreaded "cat calls" by guys, and girls. I know I am not ugly because I am constantly being complimented.

Just realizing how these statements are really not even in the range of true, makes you feel lighter, airier, and like fluff that wasn't so bad. I am amazeballs. I jotted it down for each release I had written on the paper, rereading it a time or two in my mind's eye. Then I took the "shitake list" and walked out back with a lighter in hand. I wiped my nose, and stomped a mud hole in the paper's arse, ripped the fluffer a little, screamed at the top of my lungs, and allowed myself to feel the anger, frustration, resentment of having it block me from so much in my life, and causing actual pain in my life ... then I lit the paper on fire over my fire pit ...

As the paper burnt, I allowed myself to express gratitude. I am grateful for the place you had in my life, but you no longer serve my highest self in love and light; therefore, I bid you ado. I stated, "Mom, I am grateful for you giving me life and teaching me what I did not want to be, but in love and light I let you go...." As I watched the paper burn, tears streaming, I saw the blocks dissipate into the air in love and light.

I felt lighter, so much lighter, clearer, laser-sharp focused and like the 300lb weight that once was attached to my back had finally dissipated. I felt emotionally drained, but also so fluffing excited for the road ahead because deep down, I knew this was just the very beginning.

My next step was practicing gratitude. I started what I refer to as a "gratitude jar," where I took a mason jar, cut a slit in the middle of the top, and every single day (multiple times during the day), I would write down on a small sliver of paper what I was grateful for and put it in the jar. To double up on the gratitude because it's really the magic behind accepting, and being happy right where you are, I decided to create a "gratitude journal." I wrote in my gratitude journal every single night before I laid my head on the pillow.... Why? Because there isn't anything like going to sleep in joy, feeling grateful, and dreaming beautifully, and waking the next morning on the right side of the bed, ready for the day ahead.

Before I knew it, I was watching lives of other coaches, I was drawn to three in particular – one was *super* duper expensive – I'd never have invested that kind of money to up level my life, and never ever would I ever have considered it ... but something had changed, shifted, and I realized that in order to get where I desire to be, then of course I need to be willing to invest fully in myself. To invest, to shift, to grow, expand, and love the shitakes out of myself. Well, needless to say ... I took a deep breath, pulled out my American Express, and *bam* 20k vanished just like that. I maxed out my credit card, and trusted that the Universe had my back, I also repeated affirmations such as: I am a money magnet, money comes to me with ease and flow. This only calmed my lizard, so that I could trust, believe, and know I'm finally, for the first time in my whole dang life, all in, bawz deep, on me.

When you choose to put yourself first, to surrender, and to live on the edge of your seat by stepping outside your comfort zone it's fluffing terrifying, but so dang worthy … that is when everything changes in your favor. It's also when your lizard will climb the fluffing walls, and even peel the paint. Having massive stroke symptoms, he made me ponder if the choice I made would bite me in the arse, and question whether with a brand-new baby on the way, am I sure this was the right move? I allowed myself to doubt, ponder for about 5.4 seconds before I said "Enough," and reigned him in. I let him know everything is perfectly fine, and this is when I learned the importance of tapping. I am a self-taught tapper and trust me it's pretty fluffing magical for making the lizard go back into the cave his arse came out of. Once you're all in financially, emotionally, and you have made that beautiful choice to leap, the trust and belief are what's left because that's where the lizard wants to plant seeds of doubt to get you back in the box … the safe zone, the path where you can see the outcome, but you know that in order to make shitakes happen, to make money, change is needed, and if you expect others to invest in your high-level shitake, and to take you seriously as the guru in your field, then guess what – you better be willing to do the same. Like attracts like. Therefore, if you are always buying an $11 course off Udemy to learn, shift, and grow, guess what someone is going to be willing to pay you for that beautiful knowledge? $11.11.

I started the deep dive on self-work because it was dang time to love the shitakes out of myself. Since I'd already done a few steps, the next one was accepting who I am, right where I am. In order to do this, I did some mirror work, to allow myself to see the real me instead of the distorted version of self. I complimented myself daily on one feature, one thing I saw ... "Oh, your eyes look amazing today." At first, it felt comical, silly, and just fluffing strange ... but then you start to really get into it and feel the effects. You also actually start to see yourself shift, feel yourself shift, and gazing at your eyes, you start to see the sparkle, the fire within... Pretty amazing shitakes.

This beautiful exercise also allowed me to finally step up even more ... to feel comfortable enough to go live in this private Facebook group space for the first time ever. Man, oh man ... was I terrified. The video was twenty-two seconds long, but I did it! Officially, I did it! I leapt right out into the unknown, by feeling the fear and doing it anyways. The support, the love, the compliments showered in ... I felt amazeballs, but I realized that was only just the tip of that beautiful iceberg. Each time I challenged myself to go live – to step outside the confinements of the box that once tried to contain me – I felt less terrified, and eventually I started to love it. After the first live, I started really just showing up as my beautiful, vulnerable self, just speaking my truth, giving content, and – fast forward – the next thing I know, I have 618 friends, 4,000 people on my email list. I was ecstatic! I continued to shift, to grow, by believing, leaping, and living on the edge of my seat. I started to really enjoy being of service and allowing others to hear my message. It was quite powerful.

Venturing outside the box again ... I started going live on my personal Facebook page, and drawing in more and more of an audience, then I realized as I continued to show up, to love the shitakes out of myself, and be who I am ... I started to spiritually feel the shift. No, I am not religious, nor am I not religious, but I am indeed spiritual.

My coach was on board and provided me with the insider information that I was indeed very gifted, and in all honesty, deep down I had always known because as a child, I remembered having certain knowings, feelings, and have always been super duper intuitively gifted. I have always been an empath, as well as a lucid dreamer.

Little did I know, I was called to be so much more than I'd ever imagined. However, I always had this knowing that my purpose was big ... it always felt big, and again, keep in mind – even as I write this now, it's only the beginning. I realized one day that I had a calling to go into this big-arse group of 26k members. I felt like I was either going to regurgitate, or pass out, so I had a decision to make: either step up to the challenge, and rise like the phoenix, or run with my tail between my legs in fear.... Well, before I could complete the thought, I went live, started channeling spirit, and giving intuitively guided messages to this beautiful tribe of like-minded souls. This only started my spiritual journey. I was shocked, dismayed by the words, by the beautiful way in which I channeled, and the way I felt, delivered, and just showed up. After re-watching myself, (which is scary in itself) I began to notice I didn't even look the teensiest bit nervous. This is when you know you are fluffing capable of so much more, and your adrenaline kicks in on overdrive. When you are willing to surrender – to feel the fear and do it anyways – beautiful things happen.

From there, my coaching practice has just taken off, as I continued to show up, be me, share my message, my journey, my insight, my tools, and my love for the fluffing world. I continued with my beautiful message to raise the vibration of the planet by empowering women. The first official month as my brand-spankin' new self in my coaching business was January of this year where I conducted a five-day virtual challenge… I had 98 beautiful ladies sign-up, show up, and really be all in. I had so many praises, testimonials, women who were manifesting money left and right. They were making shitakes happen, and I felt so fluffing proud. *So proud*. I can't even tell you how amazing it feels when you step in your truth and are fully aligned…. Not to mention helping others make shitake happen feels so dang good.

After the five-day challenge, I asked myself what am I going to create for these beautiful like-minded souls that desire to continue working with me? In that moment, I started thinking outside the box, and I opened a brand spankin' new group, outed myself officially to the world as an intuitive healer, mindset visionary, and bad-arse biz coach via Facebook. I also opened my brand-spankin' new group "Fearless Intuitive Babes" to the world in February, and in one month, I had 333 beautifully empowered women join my group. My marketers, my friends, my colleagues, my coach … they all were floored…. Keep in mind, this type of growth is fluffing unheard of. Most strive to have a 10 percent increase – well, mine was 250 percent. As my beautiful, fearless brand continues to grow, so do the interactions, love, and support the beautiful like-minded souls give and receive from one another. I began to realize how big what I have created even at this level really is, how many lives I'm affecting, and fluff it feels good.

Stepping outside the box, yet again I made the intuitive decision to open a VIP Group for a monthly subscription ... against the wishes of others, but I said fluff it because I don't ever fully just accept that others know better than me, so I always check in with my body, my gut, my soul self, and it felt right to launch this beautiful group against all the odds that were supposedly stacked against me....

Right off the bat, I had thirty-five beautifully empowered women take the leap, and pay $33 bucks a month in order to be part of a VIP Tribe of continuous learning.

My next launch was a big program. My first in my brand-spankin' newly branded business... a mastermind to initially test the market with my book concepts, and my own coaching abilities. I was a bit nervous, and trust me, the crazy-arse lizard was trying to climb the walls, but I always tapped, meditated, and got myself back to center... I allowed myself to really color outside the lines with my business, how I made decisions, conducted business, and it paid off big time. Not only that it always felt good, which is so dang important. I always felt like I was in integrity, and piece by piece, the mental sludge dissipated more and more... Then *bam* I had ten beautifully empowered women (which was the max I was taking this go around) sign up at 4,444 per person... that's a 44.44k month. Not to mention a few other beautiful ideas I sold putting me at over 50k for the month. I was so dang ecstatic – tears filled my eyes, I did a thirty-minute happy dance while chanting "Holy Fluffing Shitakes!" As I cried tears of joy, I began to reflect upon the short journey to here, and how all it really took was awareness, and being willing to go all in on me. Has it come with ease and flow – fluff yes.

However, one of the important things that you have to do – and I teach you a shift ton of techniques, tools, and ways to make this happen for your own dang beautiful vision – is to always check in with yourself. You have to check in and ask yourself "Is this in the highest alignment of my soul self?" If you get a tug, pinch, poke, discomfort of any kind in your body ... or the feeling of "shackles on," then guess what, it's not in alignment which means "No Go." If you get butterflies, excitement, heart palpitations, or the feeling of joy ... it's in alignment and time to move forward. This step is super crucial because if you're not in alignment, then of course whatever you manifest is often short-lived, or you'll run into the wall face first.

I knew there was no turning back, and as you can see this is only the beginning. Every single day, I allow myself to grow, shift, stretch, and evolve. The lizard who once ran my daily life on auto-pilot is now often easy to calm (takes two seconds versus the hours in the beginning), I become aware much faster, and I love who I am, where I am, and I am so dang grateful for every connection, every dollar, every client I assist, every single testimonial, and I know this is right where I'm meant to be. I crave the same for you. If you are ready to put yourself first, and be all in on you... this is the perfect book for you, and from being all in you will indeed shift, change, evolve....

Chapter Three

THE JOURNEY AHEAD...

"The best view comes from the toughest climb."
– Christie Hayden

"Pretty-Girl Bawz On"

The journey ahead is one of unconditional love, joy, and universal knowledge. In this beautiful book, you are going to discover how to "shed the shitakes," that no longer serve your highest self in order to make space mentally, physically, and emotionally for what you really desire to come into your life.

You are going to learn how to see the bigger, better, brighter picture, and be grateful for everything you currently have in your life, even the air in your beautiful lungs. The reason for this step is the fact that it's important to <u>accept where you currently are without resentment because only then can you truly decide where you want to go</u>. Only then can you strategize a plan to climb that ladder.

Within this book, you are going to learn that everything you seek starts with putting yourself first; therefore, you will realize that you always have a choice, and knowing the importance of checking in with your body before leaping into something face first will keep you from venturing off your yellow brick road. You are going to learn the importance of creating a desire list because words hold a shitake-load more meaning than we even know about. Thus, the verbiage and way you actually communicate your dreams, aspirations, and desires is super-duper important. Like attracts like; therefore, this is going to keep you from attracting more of what you truly do not desire.

By putting yourself first, you will also realize the magic already resides within you, and this is only going to help you make shitakes happen.

You are also going to discover how to color outside the lines by thinking outside of that big, beautiful, societal box. Which is super-important because no box can ever truly contain you, and you are not made to fit a mold of any sort. You are not cookie cutter; therefore, you have to be able to use your own intuition and inner guidance, in order to make decisions that are best aligned to you. Which keeps you from actually "people-pleasing," and doing shitake out of alignment... which gives results that are often short-lived and temporary at best.

You are going to learn a way to make shitakes happen. By allowing yourself to feel the fear and do it anyway. Allowing yourself to step outside your comfort zone, and live life on the edge of your seat by being present.

We are also going to dive in face first into learning the importance of boundaries, and how to set those up because, trust me, not doing so can be disastrous, have you facing burn-out, feeling overwhelmed, or – if you are like me – giving everything in your business away for free.

You are going to continuously learn ways to silence the lizard as you become more aware of when he rears his silly little head, so that you can turn your thoughts faster, with ease and flow. Which will keep you manifesting and attracting exactly what you desire into your life.

You are also going to learn brand-spankin' new tools in order to face the woman in the mirror. Which is super important in accepting and learning to love the shitakes out of who you are… whether you are 300lbs, 100lbs, or the biggest nerd in the entire freakin' world. This is not only going to keep you feeling high-vibe as fluff, but also stop you from competitor or imposter syndrome, and keep you in full alignment with your gorgeous self.

Throughout this beautiful journey, you'll have unconditional support, love, and resources at your disposal. Keep in mind, that once your eyes are open, there is no turning back … nor will you ever want to. This is just the beginning of your beautiful road to self-discovery, self-love, and really stepping into your truth in a smexy kind of way.

Together we will ignite the spark within you, and keep your fire burning. You will learn about additional ways to work with me personally in order to assure your quantum leap from where you are to where you desire to be. You can absolutely do it on your own, but ask yourself, how long have you already been trying that? It's so much faster and easier with a guiding hand.

Chapter Four

SHEDDING THE SHITAKES…

"Grow through what you go through."
– Danielle LaPorte

"Let It Go, Let It Go"

Time for a funny story. My beautiful little girl is eight months old, and she is currently standing on her own, and trying to follow in her big brother's footsteps. However, the other day, I noticed how she innately would just sing, dance, and clap even when no one was around. Just tooting her own horn, experiencing her own joy, and loving the shitakes out of life. I was flabbergasted because it proves a very solid point that when we come to this beautiful world, we intuitively already know how to have fun, to love unconditionally, and to live life for ourselves. Innately, we could care more about who is around, or watching, as we continue to live by the beat of our own dang drum. It's so fluffin' beautiful. Which brings me to the question: What the fluff happened?

Where did we go wrong, and why the heck did we decide to unlearn being free of the societal norms, to fall out of love with ourselves, to doubt our every dang decision, and not to dance to the beat of our own drum? Pretty fluffin' nutty butters, right? To start with the simplest thing, we come into the world embracing unconditional love, and we throw that out the window once we start to learn.... For example, what if as a child, you dreamt of being a rocket scientist for NASA, or a belly dancer in India, and your parents told you to pick something a bit more realistic because that isn't even in the realm of possibility.... That feeling of not being good enough, unworthy, has now been uncovered, and the shackles have officially been introduced. This is exactly what happens... we learn that there are limits, a box which we must color inside of to be considered a "good, normal girl."

However, I am here to tell you: Fluff that shitake right now. The box is an illusion created by society just to keep you playing small, and of course, safe from big bold visions, or dream-come-trues.... However, if you're on this planet, it's because you sought to live in joy, to live in adventure, to fluffing love unconditionally, and not to be shackled to a box of ideas that do not even begin to represent who you are inside.

When we love the shitakes out of ourselves, we are not bothered by the bull crap opinions, or drama of others or ourselves. We are vibrating at a higher frequency, and able to forgive, forget, and move forward without suppressing a fluffing thing. Instead we actively choose to live in joy, compassion, empathy, understanding, and gratitude.

Can you imagine what the world would be like if we all loved the shitakes out of ourselves? Everyone would appreciate everyone else, violence would be non-fluffin'-existent, and there would be no jealousy, self-loathing, narcissism, racism, sexism, and everyone could just do, and be, who and whatever the heck they desired without facing shame, guilt, or judgement. Who the heck wouldn't want to be a part of that world? A little home slice of Utopia?

The first step into making this dream a reality or creating the life you desire is "shedding the shitakes." Thus, the first activity you're going to want to do is allow yourself to first calm the lizard by tap, tappity, tapping on your left temple, right temple, your third eye. This will calm your lizard, and honestly makes him go into a state of hibernation. Right back into the cubby hole he crawled out of.

Now what you're going to want to do is take three deep breaths inhaling through your nose and holding it for the count of 5...4...3...2...1. Now exhaling out through your mouth, and as you exhale I want you to see as well as feel all of the negative energy, the stress, the worry, the expectations, the frustrations of the day leaving your body.... (Complete this process three times)

Now that you are feeling clearer, lighter, laser-sharp focused, you are ready to dive deep, face-first right into our "shed the shitake" list. This exercise is going to teach you how to let go of the shitake that you have been packing around that is no longer in alignment with your highest self. Thus, you are ready to release it from your life, in order to make room for what you truly desire.

Step 1: Jot down all of the stuff that you are letting go of (people, things, memories). Every single thing – I don't care if it's Binky made fun of your two front teeth in kindergarten and that made you feel ugly, or unworthy. Add it to the list. Keep in mind, the deeper you dive… the more you will release, the more space you will clear, and the lighter/freer you will feel. Also, there is no contest or absolute wrong way of doing this, so make sure you are aware if that lizard starts to chime in, and tap, tappity, tap him back to space.

Step 2: Allow yourself to "feel the feels." Thus, you want to make sure you're giving yourself the ability to visualize, or to go back to that spot in time when the event occurred, and really feel it … this is the only way to really process it, and free yourself from its constraints. Trust me, crying is not bad. That's some societal mumbo-jumbo, and so fluffing untrue. Crying is releasing, cleansing, and super-fluffing-healing. (Hint: If you find yourself unable to cry right away, do not fret. Don't let your lizard chime in and tell you that you are doing it wrong…. Remember, there is no wrong way. What you want to do is continue through the process, and you may have to shed the shitakes more than once, that's okay. I had to as well, and you can revisit this as often as you need.)

Step 3: Now is the time to grab your lighter (you, Firestarter, you) and take a beautiful step outside. This is where you get to read your list one last time ... allowing yourself to feel the feels, and stomp a mud hole in the list's arse, you can rip it a little or a lot, scream at the top of your lungs... and then lastly, set fire to your list. As it dissipates in love and light...

Step 4: Set your intention for the list. This is when you let the Universe know that you are grateful for the shitakes (name it) on the list, but you are releasing them in love and light as they no longer are in alignment with your highest self. Continue to watch the list dissipate, and as it floats away... visualize yourself physically releasing the load of weight you've been carrying around on your shoulders, on your back, or in your throat.

After you've officially completed the shed the shitake list, you should feel lighter, relieved, and maybe even a bit drained, or exhausted... because you've really moved a lot of energy and released shitakes that you have secretly been holding on to for decades. Keep in mind, this shift is only temporary, and you may feel bleh for a day, but you will soon notice you're going to feel fluffin' amazeballs, and high on life.

Trust me, this may sound too dang simple, and guess what, it is. However, I promise you'll resist, you won't shed it all the first go round, and will want to rinse and repeat this beautiful exercise as needed... How do I know? I've been right there. Don't believe me? Let's talk about a beautiful client.

For now, let's call her Sarah. Sarah, like many others who come to me for assistance, was super hesitant, resistant to anything that had her step outside the box she deemed her safe zone. She felt as though this exercise was not only silly, but not something she would ever do. After coaching about the importance of opening her mind, expanding her horizons, and stepping right on outside that comfort zone, and living on the edge of her seat, Sarah's resistance started to dissipate. Sarah realized that the goals, the dreams, the hopes she had weren't in that box she was currently living out of, so why the heck not give it a go. Sarah completed the "shed the shitake list," and came to our next appointment as a different person. She continued to tell me how doing it the first time was just like going through the motions, but didn't really allow her to rip out the root of the issue ... it was just surface level. Sarah told me she wasn't ready to give up on herself, as she had heard from other clients how amazing this exercise was, so Sarah did the unthinkable for herself, and repeated the exercise. This time Sarah dug deep, Sarah was all in, she made the conscious decision that she no longer wanted to play small, and was so fluffin' ready to step outside her comfy box confinements. Sarah told me that this time, "I cried, I screamed, I yelled, I stomped, I kicked rocks, and I burnt the list." This time I actually felt a huge release. Bawling, sobbing right there on the phone with me, Sarah said, "Thank you, this is so what I needed. You held space, coached me through the resistance, and I feel so much lighter, younger even, and so ready to show up as me in the world." This one exercise forever helped Sarah release things from the past that no longer served her, and allowed her to finally see a glimpse of the bigger picture.

Trust me, this exercise is fundamental.

Chapter Five

I CAN SEE CLEARLY NOW…

"It is our choices that show what we truly are, far more than our abilities."

– J. K Rowling

"Bigger, Brighter, Bolder"

The storm clouds have passed, and now you are feeling lighter, energetically, emotionally, and even physically. You may actually even feel five years younger, and ten pounds lighter. Warning: There may actually be a little pep in your step, a strut in your walk, and you may feel like dancing down every hallway.

The first step in seeing clearly is really appreciating where you are. Therefore, your next step is going to be to create a "gratitude journal." You can use any notebook, journal, or notepad that you feel drawn to, and what you are going to write is: "Thank you Universe for_____." Writing it just as it's written here is super, duper important because you want to make sure that you are writing it in past tense as if you already own it or as if it has already happened. This lets the Universe know energetically that you are ready for it. Keep in mind: Everything is energy. Also, I always highly recommend starting your daily routine off with the gratitude journal, and if possible ending the night with it because it will maintain your high vibe throughout the day and set you up for success for the next day ahead. Plus, who likes to go to bed in a bad-arse mood? Not me. "What You Desire, Desires You"

Is what you desire man's red fire? Holy Jungle Book. However, truly it's time to dream big, and really think about what is it that you'd like to manifest in your life. This could be a big smexy romance, or being a billionaire, or owning your very first Porsche. Regardless of how big or small the ticket price is, the point must be that you believe it to be possible. Therefore, it has to be in your realm of possibility, and you have to be able to believe it can really happen, or that you can make it happen.... Without that factor, it's simply an unreachable dream. Thus, you always want to start off with what you readily know or believe to be achievable. For example, "I believe I can manifest $500 in a week." Well, state your claim, and now it's time to put your motivation where your mouth is... wait, I don't think that was the saying, but you catch my drift.

Thus, the next exercise I have for you is the "desire list, and it's all about dreaming big, and realizing that anything is truly in your realm of possibility. Remember, we have unlimited potential, energy, and possibilities as we are all one. Part of that beautiful source energy, and if I may say, we are the Universe. What? Too far-fetched? Well, the truth is we are internally connected, and that way is oneness. Oneness with our highest self – Spirit, the Universe, Source, God – whatever title you feel the most called to. Knowing this at least in the back of your mind will help you realize that you can dream up anything your heart desires and know that it is indeed possible. If you are willing to take action, believe, and be open to receive ... the world is indeed your oyster.

Nothing is off limits, big or small, but the catch is you'll notice the first manifestations are things that are already believable to you. That's what you'll find yourself able to manifest with ease and flow. For example: a cup of hot java, a $20 bill, a free lunch, etc.

Step 1: You will want to start by writing everything in past tense, as though it has already shown up in your life. For example, Thank you Universe for... (the brand spankin' new White Chevy Traverse with heated leather seats).

Keep in mind, there should be no grief, no shame, or guilt around this beautiful list. Thus, if you start to notice this feeling arising, it's your lizard, and it's time for a tap, tappity, tap; meditation; yoga session; or even music to calm your subconscious mind.

Step 2: It should be any and everything you really desire to appear in your life this year.

Once your "desire list" is complete, you will want to keep it close in your room, or on your desk, in your purse, in your wallet – somewhere that you will be able to take a peek at it daily, and really visualize everything you've jotted down on your list (what color is it, what shape, what year, what features does it have, etc.).

Visualization is key to this exercise, as it not only raises your vibration, but it also lets the Universe know how seriously you desire what is on your list, and that you are ready for it. With open arms you are ready to receive, and jotting it down as though you already have it in your possession is another Jedi mind-trick for your lizard.

Another beautiful exercise I want to share with you is allowing yourself to dream out loud. Therefore, actually recording your thoughts via Siri, your iPhone, Zoom, Skype, or any recording service you currently have comfort with, and allowing yourself to hear it as you clean, cook, wash dishes, fold laundry, soak in the tub, mow the grass, or sleep. You can even get creative and record it with a beautiful meditation or sound healing going on in the background. I do this all the time. Why? Because it fluffing works, and it's healing, also you really start to believe it can happen. Remember, with what we desire, that's the whole point: being open to receive, believing, and trusting that it is indeed within the realm of possibility.

In order to fully understand the process of manifestation, we have to first discuss the "Law of Attraction." The Law of Attraction states that what we focus on is what we attract. Regardless of race, nationality, sex, or origin, we are all susceptible to the laws of the Universe. Therefore, what you think on is what grows, and where you put your focus and intention is what you will rightfully attract. For example, let's say you are depressed, in what I refer to as the "wowies me stage," feeling powerless, and claiming the role of a victim ... you will only attract more of that same rain cloud. Therefore, your thoughts are one of the most powerful things you have. They are the key to making shitakes happen or falling flat on your face with your tush in the air. They can make or break a situation ... which is why it's so dang important that you become more aware of when your lizard rears its silly head because it can lower your vibration, or worse yet, get you feeling stuck chasing your fluffing tail ... which lowers your vibe or has you attract exactly what you do not desire into your life.

The "Law of Attraction" dictates that whatever you can envision, or believe in your mind's eye to be true, can actually happen. Therefore, there really is limitless possibility... which also means limitless energy from Source (God, Spirit, The Universe), and that means that there is no limit to dreaming. Dream as big as you fluffin' like because sky's the fluffing limit, and not even then ... because there is space, Mars, Pluto even.

Honestly, the most challenging part in the acceptance of the Law of Attraction, is that you have to be very open-minded and willing as well as to clearly accept that every single decision you have ever made in your life – whether it be good, bad, right, or wrong – has molded you into the beautiful being that you are today. For many, this is a hard pill to swallow because no one likes to accept that we have always had a choice even in profound tragedies, or that our decisions played some part in the hardships we may have faced. Yes, I know the lizard's out, and feeling resistant. I've been right there so many times, and sometimes I catch myself trying to go there, but again, throughout the course of this beautiful journey you are going to see that "awareness" really is the biggest key to success. Plus, sometimes it's just so much easier to point the finger, pass the blame, or play the victim card. Trust me – been there, done that. This is why this is particularly the most difficult lesson pertaining to the Law of Attraction.

If you are reading this book, I am assuming (yes, I know all about assumptions) that you are indeed open-minded.... Thus, the best part about the Law of Attraction is the Universe always has your back. It always wants the best for you, and if you don't like the way your life is turning out, or the road you are currently on.... You always have the "free will to change it." Life is like a blank canvas, and you are the artist, so you get to choose what the finished picture looks like, as well as what method to use to get there.

Visualization is one of the top-secret tools that will help you with manifestation. Whether we believe it or not, we all have the ability to visualize in our own dang way. Whether it be lucid dreaming, seeing colors, or being able to really see yourself via meditation... visualizing is so very important, and if you do not feel you are an expert at it yet ... you can always strengthen your ability with practice. Yep! That old saying, "Practice makes perfect," also applies to manifestation.

Let's say you want to manifest a million dollars this year. The first step you want to take when using visualization to manifest the life you desire is to see that million-dollar version of yourself. Thus, what does the million-dollar version of you look like, dress like, eat like, spend time doing? Where does the million-dollar you live? Is it a one-story or two-story home? Do you have a housekeeper, a nanny, a cook? Are you in a gated community? What brands do you wear? What type of car do you drive, what color is it? Really go there, and visualize it... jot it all down, draw it if you'd like.... Ask yourself what your husband does for a living, and how many beautiful children do you have? Are you traveling non-stop? Are you exercising? The more descriptive you get, the more likely you are to believe it on a subconscious level which means the more likely it is to appear with ease and flow. Keep in mind, the key is believing at your core that it is real, can be true, and that it really can fluffing happen.

Trust me, I know if your lizard is out... this may sound way too dang easy, even bizarre. However, let's talk about another client, named Marisa. Marisa was brand-spankin' new to manifestation, the law of attraction, and to concepts outside the realm of the lizard. She was open-minded, but resistant. She desired change, to make more money in her business, and to really start to manifest the life she desired. She desired more clients, vacations, a brand-spankin' new home, and a car. She desired to live her life in joy. However, what had gotten her to this current stage was not allowing her to grow, and like many others, she struggled. She found it hard to step outside that box because the lizard would climb the walls, and anxiety would begin. After deep breathing, I had Marisa complete the "shed the shitake list," and she felt clearer, lighter, more focused. She actually responded to me the next day with "Okay, that felt amazing. What's next?" Chuckling, I explained the next step is to create a desire list… and before I could get the words out, she goes, "Oh trust me, I have a bazillion of those." Resistance. I laughed and said, "Well, this one is a bit more specific, and in a completely different format." I gave her a moment, and she said "Ohhh, okay. Let's do it." She created the desire list, and felt sky high because of course dreaming up the life you desire, and all the beautiful things in it, will only raise that vibration. Not to mention it's fun to allow yourself to dream big. The next step was creating the "successful version of herself that had the clients, vacationed, and lived the life in joy" that she desired. This one was so easy for her because she was already feeling the shift … the changes, but still there was resistance. "Well, I don't know how a successful me dresses, looks like, eats like because I've never been there." I giggled, and helped calm the lizard by meditation, tappity tap tapping, and then we tried again. I asked her about the fashion that inspired her, had her close her eyes, and tell me what her successful millionairess self would dress like. Without hesitation, she began to rattle off even the most intricate details of what that looked like. She began to dive deeper and deeper… creating this beautiful visualization, and throwing out, "You know, also I'd have three dogs and they would all have dog beds with therapeutic cushions," etc., chuckling internally, but loving every dang moment of her visualization. She left feeling as though she was walking on clouds – even her walk had changed. She walked with more confidence, more belief, more knowing that her dreams really were possible. Skip ahead a few more sessions, and Marisa was now living her life in joy and bliss, was traveling, and had manifested five new clients within a span of two months. She was on fire, and the money was just flowing in because she was doing the deep "inner work," and had cleared space for what she really desired to make way.

Proof that if you allow yourself to just go there ... to feel the fear and do it anyway ... to stop resisting, and just give it a try ... to step outside the confinements of that box ... you too can make shitake happen in your own life. It really is that simple, but we often like to overanalyze it, overthink it, and complicate the shitakes out of it by resisting, breaking it down, and this is one reason why we continue to chase our tail.

The second visualization activity I want to share with you is a vision board. Vision boards are super powerful in they are constant reminder of what you desire, and by being able to actually see it on paper, you are able to really believe it. Which is why visualization is so dang powerful, and vision boards are just one more tool for your beautiful bag. Vision boards are created by searching the web, photo albums, magazines, or newspapers for pictures of words, items, trips, feelings, or even people you'd like to manifest this year.

This visualization technique is for everyone but is super helpful for anyone that struggles with actually seeing the picture in their mind's eye and needs a bit more solidity. This is what I often refer to as a "Jedi mind-trick." Keep in mind, the big secret to the vision board is really selecting words, pictures, items, people that represent the way you'd like to feel this year ... and I am hoping for you that's joy, bliss, excitement, and love.

Step 1: Set your intentions. What do you desire? What do you need? What do you value? And how do you want to feel when everything you place on the vision board starts to manifest into your life? When thinking of the feelings, be sure to choose single, emotional words like free, open, joy, etc. Write them all down.

Step 2: Gather your supplies. They could include: blank journal, art book, notebook, canvas, poster board, shadow box, or even a corkboard. You'll also want to purchase glue, pins, markers, paint, colorful or plain paper. Next, you'll want to gather photos of you, your family, magazines, newspapers, or print online items your heart desires

Step 3: Create a Comfortable Space. You can light candles to set the mood, burn incense, gather your crystals, create a crystal grid, or even play relaxing music that will allow you to set the perfect intention while being high vibe as fluff. You will want to make sure you are comfortable, and laser-sharp focused about what it is you truly desire to manifest in your life this year.

Step 4: Find images and words that draw you in and represent your theme for the year. What would you like to feel, to be, to see, to have? Ask yourself, and then sort through the online space, magazines, or newspapers to find phrases and emotionally charged words that match your description.

Step 5: Now sort through your images and choose the ones you are the most drawn to. How do you know? Hold the imagery in your hand, and ask yourself, "Is this of my highest intention?" What does your body say? Your gut say? Your intuition say? You may hear no, or see the word no. You may also feel weight, a tug, or a pull in your chest, or discomfort in your gut ... which would also mean no. For yes, you can also see, hear, feel butterflies in your stomach, heart palpitations, or sense joy, or excitement.

Step 6: It's time to find a place in your beautiful journal, art book, notebook, poster board, or corkboard for the pictures and phrases you felt the most drawn too. Anything that is left-over or doesn't fit, you can save for a later time.

Step 7: Now you want to put your vision board somewhere you can see it daily. As seeing it is what helps you visualize it, and helps your subconscious believe it as true ... which again is a Jedi mind-trick that helps bring the items, people, feelings, and trips into your life with ease and flow. Keep in mind, this is a visual reminder of what you desire to manifest in your life this year.

After completing this beautiful vision board, and placing it somewhere you can see it daily whether it be on your desk, in your office, on your counter ... it will continue to provoke that beautiful dream come true, and this is where the real magic begins. This is indeed where everything starts to work in your favor because your thoughts and your intentions are super-duper powerful, especially in manifestation.

Chapter Six

EVERYTHING STARTS WITH YOU...

"You are everything that you dream of."
– Nekked

"Ignite the Flame"

First things first: Stop worrying about what everyone else thinks, or says. Their opinions about you, your life, and the choices you have made really do not matter. The first step in moving forward is accepting right where you are, and the next step that we are about to discuss is putting yourself first.

Remember, you hold all of the keys to your own destiny. You get to decide what color it will be, will there be stars, will there be crystals, will there be incense, will there be furniture, or a lot of like-minded people? All of these beautiful choices are yours, and yours alone. That's the best part about putting yourself first, you get to own your shitakes, and live life on the edge of your seat in joy for yourself ... surrounded by the ones that you love.

Everything starts and ends with you. Therefore, it is super important that you appreciate just how significantly unique you are, and that there is not another being in the whole Universe quite like you. Yes, we may all be talented, gifted, and even share gifts... however, no one will ever show up like you do, with your beautifully unique personality, or even think thoughts the way that you do. Thus, you are super freakin' unique, and you are all you will ever be, so that's why it's so important to start embracing it now and start putting yourself first. You are indeed a priority.

But, but, but ... No buts (my anaconda says no ... teasing). However, truly no excuses, because excuses are bull crackers. Your time is now, and you are indeed a fearless, intuitive babe. You are ready to step right on up into your truth and slay like a fluffing warrior princess. Know it, believe it, breathe it, and envision yourself as Xena with a bad-arse selenite sword. (Too much?) You have to start seeing yourself in your truth, in your highest light, and one way to start doing that is with affirmations.

An affirmation is simply a phrase, or saying, that supports and encourages progression, or the intention needed. For example, the first affirmations I would suggest as you start to put yourself first and swing in like a wrecking ball ... are self-love affirmations. Affirmations often get a bad name, but here's the deal – they really do work. It's all about selecting a couple and repeating them in your mind until you fully believe and accept them. Welcome to the Christie Brainwash. This is how you make them work. Pick your area of least satisfaction currently, and since you're just beginning your journey of self-discovery ... I would choose self-love. Then you pick the two or three affirmations that stand out the most to you, and repeat them, jot them down, and place them on a post-it on your car visor, in your desk drawer at work, in your pocket, or on your mirror at home – anywhere that will remind you.

Here are a few of my favorite affirmations for clients beginning on their journey:

- I am open to receive and give abundant amounts of love.
- I am open to receive all of the good that life has to offer me.
- I am highly intellectual, beautiful, and loving.
- I am overflowing with joy, vitality, and energy. I am unstoppable.
- I acknowledge that my own self-worth and my confidence is soaring.
- My efforts are being supported by the Universe, and my dreams are manifesting right before my own eyes.
- I am love, love is me, I love every single part of me.
- I am everything that I dream of, and the Universe has my back.

The key to affirmations is repetition, but also really feeling the emotion around what you are saying. Believing is indeed receiving. The more open you are to receive, the more willing you are to believe. At the beginning, it may feel awkward or even as though you are faking it till you make it, *but* as you continue to repeat the mantras over and over again in your mind you will start to shift and realize that this is actually your truth.

The next step in putting yourself first is really being "all in, bawz deep" on you. Thus, being willing to step outside your comfort zone which – you guessed it – will indeed feel uncomfortable. You have to be willing to speak your truth, as your voice ... your message is meant to be heard, and not doing so is being selfish. Keep in mind, putting yourself first is indeed not selfish – it's actually quite the opposite, selfless, because you are willing to do the work needed to be of your highest light and vibration in order to be of service to others. Who the heck could disagree with that?

Next, it's time to do the things you love. What the heck is that? Well as human beings whom care so deeply, love so unconditionally, and are so dang heart-centered ... we often sacrifice what we desire for the good of others. Thus, we deny ourselves the people, the friends, the parties, the romances, the experiences that we really would feel the most alive having. Which is pretty nutty butters, right? However, the intention is so beautifully pure, but and this is a *big* but ... by denying our self such joy we are low-vibing ourselves, suppressing shitakes, and letting ourselves down. Doesn't have quite the same ring to it now, does it?

Thus, ask yourself, "What do I find the most joy in doing? Going to a movie, out to a dinner, for a walk in the park, getting my nails done, or taking a vacation in Mexico?" Whatever you find the most joy in doing ... even if it's miniscule in the realm of things, it's time to make time to *do* it. Remember, we are putting you first. Therefore, no excuses, like I am just too busy.... Since now you are considered quite the priority, book yourself an appointment on your own dang calendar, and for fluff's sake, it's about time.

It's time to break your people-pleasing, putting-everyone-before-yourself ways, and if you are reading this book, I can almost guarantee you do this with someone in your life. It's time for the tables to turn, and for you to start treating yourself as you do others. Remember that golden rule we all grew up learning about in school ... "Treat others the way you desire to be treated?" Well I say fluff that ... treat yourself the way you desire to be treated, and then guess what, like attracts like.... Therefore, you will attract others treating you as you wish. "Ah ha!" Time to love the shitakes out of yourself, so that you attract only those that will do the same.

Time to make way for Princess Me. (Okay, so maybe I stole that and then ... made my own version of it from Aladdin. I do it often. It's who I am. I own the shitakes out of being a nerd, as should you if you knew that before I even stated it.) Now it's time to make time for you. Make time for yourself to meditate, shoot the shtuff, clear your mind, get grounded, do yoga, workout, cook divine food, or sip a glass of Chardonnay. Whatever tickles your fancy. I don't care if it's only twenty minutes a day. This is what I like to refer to with clients as "me time." This is when you have an uninterrupted amount of time just for yourself. To de-stress, declutter, get grounded, inspired, motivated, and back to your high-vibe arse state.

It's also time to stop making light of bad fluffing jokes. What I mean by this is ... it's time to quit being the butt of a joke and laughing about it when internally you really want to bust out in snotty booger tears. It serves no purpose to allow this shitake to continue, and it's self-deprecating. Also, stop making jokes about your weight to cover up the way you really feel about yourself. It's horse shtuff and you know it. I mean this in a loving way, but if you make jokes about yourself to hide your pain ... you are suppressing it, faking it, wearing a "mask of many colors," and trust me, that's not the road you want to go down. You are headed down a much more glorious, self-fulfilling path. I am totally guilty ... I have been there making jokes about my new baby weight, and about my Italian stallion nose ... however, internally each time, it felt like a needle directly to the heart. Inside no one could see, so I'd laugh with the best of them to hide the pain. This did not serve any purpose, but to fit in with the cookie-cutter jerk-faces (in love and light) that would make jokes about someone in that way anyhow.

What you tell yourself or refer to yourself as on a daily basis has a shift ton of power over what you think, manifest, and the energetic vibration you share. Thus, these small jokes about your own insecurities may seem harmless, but they actually do the exact opposite of affirmations. Thus, they make you believe bad shtuff about yourself – lies about yourself.

Another piece to putting yourself first is really allowing yourself to be open to receive love, money, and high-vibe frequencies. For example, if someone says "Wow, what a beautiful voice." Do you say, "Thank you, yours is nice too"? I bet you do or have. This is a big fluffing no-no. Seems harmless enough right? Well, it's your way of avoiding accepting the compliment. "Ah ha!"

The correct response is just "Thank you," (and "You're welcome" if you're the Rock) and trust me ... from one non-accepter to another this takes practice ... shift tons of practice, and sometimes I still am guilty of it. Therefore, don't beat yourself up about it if you do it, just correct the verbiage, and move forward with your day. The key is again awareness of what you are doing, and why. When you start to be more consciously aware of what you are thinking, saying, and responding with ... you will start to turn it around with more speed, ease, and flow.

Nextly, we need to nip in the bud the comparison issues. *Yep*! Guilty over here! (Two hands in the air). I used to compare myself to Joe, Shmoe, and his big toe. Wahahah! Okay, so I did indeed compare myself to celebrities, other skinny, gorgeous women, other coaches, and healers.... Trust me when I tell you it served no purpose but to make me feel like shitakes. I was self-inflicting internal wounds. Honestly, imagine cutting yourself on the inside, and that's exactly what it was. I used to say, "Well, I cannot ever do that since I have this big fluffing nose. I cannot ever wear that since my boobs are the size of my head. Why can't I be like her, how come I don't have blah, blah, blah ..." and the nasty comparisons continue on.

First off, as you can see ... it does nothing but make you feel bad about yourself, so why the fluff even do it? Well, apparently, many of us like pain, and we like to self-inflict it whenever we feel the urge ... isn't this what sadists or dominants do? However, they have a bad reputation ... we don't think so highly of them via society's rules ... *but* it's perfectly okay to go around cutting yourself internally, and comparing yourself to unrealistic standards.... Again, more horse shtuff.

Comparing yourself to others is the fastest way to lower your vibe, zap your energy, and take the fun out of life. Stop worrying about what everyone else is doing, thinking, feeling, and stay in your own lane, bay-bee. It's time for you to show up as your gorgeous authentic self, and let it all hang out. Seriously, though it's time for you to be the person you are inside, and to let your light shine. (I'm gonna let it shine) No one should ever be able to snuff it out. My old saying is "Don't be afraid to be the only light in a dark room." You are more than enough. You are more special than you give yourself credit for, and comparison only dims that gorgeous light the world needs more of. So, quit that shitake now.

The next exercise is super-duper important, as it's all about forgiving yourself for anything you may have done in the past. This is about letting yourself know that those screw-ups were nothing more than lessons, and you are indeed going to fluff up again, but you always fall forward. Therefore, you want to stop yourself from shame, blame, and guilt because there really is nothing to be guilty, shameful, or blameful for. You quite simply made a choice, that had a different outcome than what you imagined. Therefore, you forgive yourself, and you let it go. Do not, I repeat *do not* drag this bag of bull crap around with you because it does not serve your highest self and will only bring you down to shitake levels. Plus, you'll have to do another "shed the shitake list."

Now, in order to forgive yourself, I have this beautiful application other than the "shed the shitake list" that will allow you to do so. First, you'll need access to YouTube, and you'll want to type in "Ho'oponopono - Thank You I Love You – Sushumna." (Keep in mind, I own no rights to this song). However, this is super-fluffing-healing, and there are so much data to show how effective *Ho'oponopono* is in allowing yourself to heal, forgive, and to extend your life. Yep, no shitakes. During this Kundalini rising meditation, I want you to think about the things you have been carrying around, and actually forgive yourself. Trust me, before long, you will be singing along. This beautiful meditation will serve as the point of letting go, forgiving yourself, and rising above. Don't believe me? Try it.

Always know you are indeed everything you dream of, and it's so dang important for you to love who you are, where you are, and where you are going. Forgive yourself, love yourself, and know that you will always rise like the phoenix from the ashes because you are a fearless warrior princess, and that's just what you do. Believe it.

Chapter Seven

UNLEASH THE MAGIC WITHIN YOU…

"You were born with the ability to change someone's life. Don't ever waste it."

– Christie Hayden

"Magical as Fluff"

The magic has always been within you. It's always been a keen part of your being, in the inner workings of you. It may have laid dormant for some time, due to you locking it away or hiding it because it wasn't perceived as acceptable. Remember, when we first came into this world we already carried our gifts and unconditional love, and then as we began to learn… we also began to confine ourselves.

To inherit beliefs that were never ours, and to make ourselves smaller so that the rest of the world didn't feel so threatened... so that we could just "fit in" the box with the rest of society. Little did we know that by doing this, we have really and truly shackled ourselves.

Thus, in order to unleash the magic within you, you must first really open yourself up to receive. The first step is to put your hands in the air palms up toward the sky and repeat after me. *"I am open to receive what is in my highest good, or better. Thank you, thank you, thank you."* Palms down and you have now opened the gates to receiving exactly what you are prepared for.

Your next question is probably, "Well, how the heck do I know what my gift is, and how the heck do I unleash it for the world?" Well, first I totally understand this question, as not too long ago I pondered it myself. However, this is a *big* deal because this can be the deciding factor in whether or not you live a happy, fulfilled, blissful life. It's a deciding factor in how you show up, what you offer, and how you are indeed of service to the world. Every single person is born with unique valuable gifts to share with the world. However, it's so easy to overthink it, overanalyze it, and chase after your purpose for decades. Let's not do that and let me tell you a beautiful secret.

Ready? How you discover your purpose, is by making a choice, and doing it. What? Yep, it's that simple. In order to discover what you love, and what sets your heart on fire, all you have to do is be willing to try things on. Fluff! Have fun with it. Like a kid in a candy store getting to try all of their favorite treats, or a girl in a clothing store getting to try on any outfit her heart desires. It's the same exact scenario here. You get to try things on that feel good, and when it starts feeling shifty you let it go and make another "feel good choice." Therefore, like we discussed earlier in the book, you want to always check in with your body, and ask which direction serves your highest self ... then *go, run, leap*. It's time to try shift on, and it's super important that you allow yourself to play. Keep in mind, that the answers already reside within you, and they will come out all in "divine timing," but how you can expedite the process is by doing. Thinking will do nothing but allow you to dream, get frustrated, and waste endless hours you cannot get back ... but doing will allow you to have fun, to live, and to really experience the gifts life has to offer.

When I found my calling, I actually was just trying a ton of shitakes on, and bam ... once I surrendered, and decided to go all in bawz deep on myself, everything has just fallen into place, as it will for you too. However, it's the leap – not knowing the outcome, and trusting that the Universe does indeed have your back – that is the scariest test. When you are willing to surrender, to leap into the unknown, and live on the edge of your seat ... you will start to notice suggestions, opportunities, and amazing things coming your way. Don't believe me – try it. See if divine downloads, opportunities, and open doors don't start to happen.

For example, is there a book (hint, hint wink, wink), a course, a mentor, or coach showing up consistently on your feed, or that you are drawn to ... like a moth to a flame, or two magnets connecting. If so, that's a *huge* arse sign that you may be being guided to leap in that direction. Always check in with your highest self, and that beautiful intuition, but Spirit always shows us signs.

Regardless of where you are, where you start, or where you end up on your journey, always do everything to the best of your ability. Always show up with the intention of being of service to others, and not for the money. When you are in it just for the money, that is when you are out of alignment, and you'll notice you are going to manifest nothing more than desperation, scarcity, and lack of what you really desire.

Therefore, it is very important to heed the warning, and make sure your intentions are right, because every step you take leads you to the beautiful path you are meant to be on, and you always want to put your best foot forward. Keep in mind that financial abundance comes with ease and flow once you are in alignment with your highest self and showing up to be of service to others.

Another important lesson when unleashing your magic is to make sure you are not reinventing the wheel. Why fix something that is not broken, and why not see what others are doing, and how they are showing up … noticing if it's effective. Now this does not mean go copy their shtuff, mimic their personality, or be their stunt double.... This does mean to find out what programs they are using, what format they are finding the most effective, and doing your research on where to look for your soul clients, especially if they are in the same market/network as you.

Don't be afraid to co-create. What does that mean? Don't be afraid to ask for help, to accept assistance, or to join in on a mastermind, a blog, a group, a live stream, or even a podcast. Don't be afraid to show up as you, and sure as heck don't allow yourself to feel intimidated because not only do we all put our pants on the same way, but you are a beautifully radiant light all on your own. Own that shitake, show up, and know that you've got all of the magic within you.

Another key to unleashing your magic is to make sure you are indeed always seeing the glass as half full. Therefore, you are not letting that lizard pop in and sabotage your thoughts. Trust me, he can be a pretty sneaky fellow. Thus, you want to assure that you are indeed always seeing the positive in the situation, being optimistic, and really giving others the benefit of the doubt without allowing yourself to become compromised. Do not, for any reason at all, lay down and be the doormat for people to wipe their shifty feet. Trust me, I have been there ... so many times, and honestly it was the toughest lesson for me to learn because I care so deeply and see the beautiful possibilities in everyone. Which is a gift; however, without boundaries (which we will talk about soon) it can turn into more of a curse in that you are often sought after for being too kind, too caring, and others if you allow them like to use you as a doormat on which they wipe their dirty-arse feet. This is a horrible experience, and I just finally last month, after falling forward into the same trap two hundred and sixty-nine times, learned my lesson. Sometimes we have repeat lessons, which is why in the beginning of this book we discussed chasing your tail. This is when you continue to be right where you are, stagnant, and learning the same vicious lesson over and over again ... until you finally, really get it. It's also important to realize it's never a mistake, but a lesson. We will always have lessons to learn – that is part of our evolution here on Planet Earth – and we will always stretch, grow, shift, and change. There will always be this transformation to bigger, better, and brighter things, so keep that in mind as you continue on your path toward glory.

The key is showing up as your authentic, beautiful self, and sharing vulnerably your message without expectation, but with the intention that you are being of service to others. Helping them learn from you, with you, and through you. This is an important reminder ... that there should not be a tie to the outcome, but more of an intention. For example, I am going to show up as my authentic self, sharing my beautiful message to help raise the vibration of the planet, and in doing so I know I will be successful because the Universe does indeed have my back. Not to mention I am amazing, I am worthy, I am inspirational, and I am so ready. Now it's time to really make shitakes happen, and how you ask? By showing up as you. By showing up, whether it be via blogging your story, or inspirations, or even bits and pieces of both, or maybe you show up on a live talk with a theme. For example, just yesterday I showed up live in a group and talked about the importance of boundaries, and how to implement them in your own life. I also included my own experience with no boundaries, and the struggle to implement them. This was super beneficial and landed me twenty-five more followers, as well as three paying clients. This is how it really does work. Showing up as your authentic, vulnerable self, and taking action.

It's also important that you find out via market research where your people are hiding out. Cue the lights for the "soul client" description. In this exercise, I want you to tell me what your ideal client/customer looks like. What do they enjoy doing? How old are they, are they single, married? Do they enjoy cooking, the outdoors, or do they enjoy video games? What sets their heart on fire, what inspires the shitakes out of them, and what do they find themselves lost doing? Ask yourself, do they own, rent, or live with family? Are they broke as fudge cookies, and barely scraping by, middle class, or are they semi-wealthy, and just not fulfilled? Paint this beautiful picture for yourself, so that you can connect the dots to where your soul clients might be hanging out. Plus, it's super insightful.

Next, it's time to find your beautiful clients. You can do this by searching groups on Facebook – which I highly recommend – you can do this by word of mouth referrals, you can do this by posting on sites that they'd be drawn to. You can even do this by attending the places they love to go. There are so many ways to really find your soul clients, but first you have to uncover who they are, and where they might be, so I would definitely do this exercise to help you uncover those cues.

Also, it's important to keep in mind, as you continue on your path to greatness, that you are responsible for what you say and do, but you are not responsible for how others choose to react, respond, or reply. Remember that their response is on them. Their deflection often happens when we trigger others with something we share, and they decide to throw an upper cut, or a virtual fluff you in the mix. The most important thing is that you know it's not you, it's not personal, it's them. They were triggered, which is a beautiful opportunity for them to dig deep and find out why... to pull out the roots, heal, and let it go, but remember that's on them, and that is indeed their lane. Stay in yours.

Which leads me to my next point: What others think of you has nothing to do with you, and everything under the sun to do with them. Again, a deflection or defense mechanism that occurs when someone is triggered – or in other words, not ready for what was shared.

This leads me to another key point that part of unleashing your gifts and showing up for yourself with confidence is validating yourself. If you are often looking to others for compliments, advice, or a pat on the back ... you might just be a sinking ship. The reason behind that is you will grow addicted to outside validation, and you will always doubt your own inner guidance. This is "no *bueno*," and only leads you on a downward spiral to an identity crisis because you will start to think everything you thought was a lie. By seeking validation from others, you are chasing it, and you have no control over it ... over their mood, their thoughts, their intentions, and guess what? Sometimes they up and disappear … then what happens? That downward, Alice-in-Wonderland rabbit hole appears. Trust me, that is not the route you desire to take. When someone compliments, as you learned earlier, it's perfectly fine to say "Thank you," but do not feed into it, and do not – for the love of all you hold dear – get yourself caught up in the praise.

When unleashing your magic to the world, always check in with your highest self, again by asking why. Why do you desire to do this, what is motivating you, is it because you are being called to, is it because you are jealous, is it because you are angry, or is it because it sounds like it would be fun? Always check in and ask yourself because this is how you are going to become aware of if you are in alignment with your highest self. This will also help you see if the intention behind your actions is pure, or if it's your lizard rearing its silly head. Keep in mind, we always want to act out of our soul self and stay in integrity to who we are. Therefore, doing something that could hurt, belittle, or bring harm in any way is definitely not okay.

Trusting your intuition and gut instinct is going to be so very important when you are unleashing your beautiful self to the world and showing up with your bad-arse message for the world. Therefore, if you feel a nudge in the gut, or a pull in the chest … it's time to listen. To get silent, and to allow yourself to connect to Spirit, so that you are able to allow your inner compass to guide your way. I am sure you can recall past lessons where in hindsight, you wish you would have listened to that nudge in your belly. Yep! That is your intuition. You can continue to practice strengthening it even more so by meditating, doing yoga, Reiki sessions, and listening to sound healings. This allows you to tune in to Source, and to expand, shift, and grow.

Chapter Eight

COLOR OUTSIDE THE LINES

"You get in life what you have
the courage to ask for."

– Oprah

"Outside of the Box Thinking"

In this chapter, we learn the importance of outside of the box thinking, and how it can serve your highest good. For example, I have always been someone who colors outside the lines. Who defies gravity, rebels against a system, and has always believed all you need is love. That's right, a hippy and old soul in my own dang right. Pretty proud of it because love makes the world go around, and dang, don't we need more of it.

When we start to strategize, whether it be for a brand-spankin' new house, a brand-spankin' new business as an entrepreneur, or how to manifest $500 in a week ... it all needs to start with being in alignment with your highest self. The check-in should start to become routine; therefore, you should always ask is this of the highest light or better for myself....

Next, you should always allow yourself to fantasize. Not in a pornographic type of way, but as in, if anything were possible, any career field at all, what would you desire the most to do? Would you like to run away with Roadshow Bob, join the excursion in Egypt, or sail across the Caribbean Sea? Allow yourself the fantasy because it brings you joy, hope, and guess what – sometimes it's where you're headed. Our fantasies often start as young adolescents, daydreaming, and remember at this age we are still intact with our highest self, our purest light ... that quite possibly you will be a Roadshow Bob Pirate that attends excursions in Egypt. (Ha ha) Well, heck remember anything is possible, and that really is the point. Fantasies are indeed a small vision into who we are, what we enjoy, and more connected to our calling than we know or will ever willingly admit. Many of us use excuses like "Oh, I know this is silly," or "I know this sounds stupid, but I have always dreamed of being an international hot dog eater. Please hold while I laugh." However, the point is no idea is ever stupid. No idea or dream is ever too big, too small, or impossible. Heck, not even the word impossible is impossible. Thus, put your pretty-girl bawz on, and always be willing to leap, even if it is a Roadside Bob excursion.

How you ask? Well your job, gorgeous, isn't to know the

how, but to know the what. What you will be doing, what will get you to that point. The how will come in divine timing when you are open and ready to receive. In order to open yourself up to receive the how – the evidence, the fruits of your labor – you now must be open to asking. Thus, in order to receive, you must ask. Refer back to the desire list exercise, and always ask in past tense, as if it's already happened. "Thank you, Universe, for _____," and remember, the more specific you get, the more likely it is for your subconscious to fully believe it as being possible, and therefore the more likely it is to appear in your life with ease and flow.

Coloring outside the lines as a school age adolescent was first always about being a leftie for me, but then it became about what can I get away with. Yep. I have always been highly fluffin' intelligent, a risk-taker, a floater, and a creative guru. I have always leapt on the opportunity to showcase my ability to color outside the lines.

For example, as a young girl I loved to draw, to write, and to create. Well, one time when I was about eight years old ... I didn't have paper (shock, shock), nor did I own a coloring book, or crayons, and I knew better than to ask my mom for it. So, my creative genius came up with an epic fluffing plot. I decided I was going to get rocks of different shades – because I didn't have chalk either – and that I would draw on the brick to our garage. Well, first off what a fluffing brilliant idea! Right? After gathering the supplies, and coloring till my heart was content ... my mom came outside and boy, was she mad. I didn't sit down for weeks;

however, people that would walk by would complement the artistry, how different it was, and dang, did that feel good. It was so worth the beating, and it's this thinking that I have innately always carried. This thinking that makes me unique, different, and it's this thinking that will do the same for you. Keep in mind, that you want to always feel the fear, and do it anyway. Show up for yourself and see where it leads you… promise it'll be somewhere better than you ever even imagined possible. Don't believe me? Try it.

An important part of coloring outside the lines is knowing the difference between expectation and intention. I hear so many gurus that say having expectations is a great motivational tool for success … *well* … I will kindly have to agree to disagree because expectations do nothing but add unnecessary pressure to already pressurized situation, as well as they can often lead to feeling disappointed, ashamed, and guilty. Which of course we want no part of.

Expectations are really a way of giving up your power and putting it in someone or something else's hands sprinkled with glitter, sparkles, hope. Expectations are attachments to the outcome. If you are in alignment, you most likely don't know the outcome, as it's unknown. Therefore, if you set an unrealistic expectation that doesn't come true… it can leave you feeling frustrated, like a failure, unworthy, and you'll be back to square one.

For example, let's say you are headed to an amazing meeting with a brand-spankin' new client, and you are leaving a few minutes later than you originally scheduled because you expect you will find a parking spot super close to the meetup. Well, upon your arrival there isn't an empty spot in sight, and you actually have to park two blocks away. How would you feel? Honestly. You would probably be ticked off, frustrated, upset, beating yourself up about leaving later than expected, blaming the Universe for not following through, and not having your back, and you'll just be in a grumbly mood energetically ... Guess what this does? It then has you miss out on the client because energetically, you didn't vibe – sending you into an even more raging fit of "fluff you, world." Then what happens next? You get back to your car, and lo and behold there is a beautiful parking ticket on your front windshield.... At this point, your lizard is climbing the Eiffel tower, and you are fluffing cursing, ranting, and on a downward spiral to the abyss. No *bueno* indeed. This is why setting expectations often has you feeling fluffed, stuck, and in overwhelm. Also, I want you to notice that once you are vibing at that low place, that all you attract is more low-vibe bull crap. (Hint: the loss of the client, the parking ticket.)

Now let's discuss intention. Intentions are something you are planning or would really like to do. Thus, it's all about using your laser-sharp focus, and proposing a plan of action. Thus, our intention is fully on our focus, the plan of action, making shitakes happen – it's not tied to the outcome in any way. That is where you want to live. It frees yourself from having to fear loss, unworthiness, or getting low-vibe as fluff. It allows you to use your energy to manifest mindfulness toward your efforts. Simply put, an intention is an impulse, or divine download that gets your creative juices flowing, and allows your energy to surge. Now let's use the same example, but this time we set the intention with our laser-sharp focus that we find a parking space close to the meetup. Thus, upon arriving, we notice an empty spot in a lot that is across the street. Instead of being upset that it wasn't front row parking, you find yourself grateful and thanking the Universe for having your back. Thus, only maintaining your high vibe. Guess what happens next? You slay in the meeting and book a brand-spankin' new client. Life is amazing, and on the stroll back to your car, you are thanking the Universe for all of the amazing opportunities gifted to you.

Trust me, this lesson can be a tricky one. Let's talk about another client named Naomi. Naomi is a beautifully successful client in her own dang right. She's already making a lot of waves in the ocean, but feels unfulfilled in her corporate-America position, and often dreams of being an entrepreneur. What stops her? Fear, the lizard, and going for broke by losing her reliable salary. Naomi completed the exercises, and had plenty of ah-ha moments, and decided to take the leap "all in" bawz deep on herself ... but it didn't come without resistance or struggle. One of her biggest struggles was when it came to setting expectations over intentions. For example, Naomi would state I expect to see six-figure months within six months in my own business as an entrepreneur. Of course, three months would come and go ... Naomi would be right at the mid-line of what she expected, and instead of seeing fifty-thousand months as amazing, she would be like, "Well, shitake, I didn't hit my goal again, and now my whole dang business is going down in flames. I should have listened to my lizard. I should have just stayed where I was, blah, blah, blah." (I'll spare you the downward spiral.) She would choose to go down the rabbit hole into the dark abyss because she felt like she wasn't doing well, and at the core she not only had a tie to the outcome, but she was still holding on to this core belief that she wasn't good enough for six figure months. *Bingo*. How did she realize it? By going there, feeling it, and allowing herself to spiral out of control (which was the much more challenging route to where she desired to go, but it still led her to the answer.) She was able to see, "Holy shitake. I am not making the six-figure months because I keep setting expectations that I don't even believe or feel worthy of." (Jackpot.) Once you have that "ah-ha," that epiphany, that gold nugget of information, you then take it back through the process of "shedding the shitakes," and let it go in love and light.

Naomi also realized that setting expectations to an outcome was not the way to do business – or life even – because we should be present in the moment, taking action, making shitakes happen.... Therefore, we shouldn't cap our own possibilities. Needless to say, the next month in business Naomi hit 99k right under the six figures she desired, and this time she celebrated. She was dang happy, seeing the glass half full, and this is the most important part.

Remember to always celebrate your wins; even the tiniest of wins is important, and worthy of celebration. You can celebrate posting your first blog with pie, cake, candy, a fluffin' Netflix episode, whatever tickles your fancy, and as you continue up the ladder, each celebration should be bigger in reward, and equally just as satisfying. Life is worth living, and it's worth celebrating.

Thus, as you discovered via Naomi's story, another key component in the art of coloring outside the lines is really accepting that you may not know the outcome, nor should you as it takes the fun out of it. However, you do know that it's going to be one heckuva process because if you are anything like me, you are going to sample every color in the box. Thus, have fun! This is really where you are in alignment – this is really when the magic happens, the switch flips – and just trust that the Universe will bring into flower exactly what you are desiring. Also, always be willing to be present. Don't allow that lizard to veer you too far off the path of joy, and make sure you're always practicing your awareness.

Chapter Nine

FEEL THE FEAR AND DO IT ANYWAY

"She was afraid of heights, but she was much more afraid of never flying."

– Atticus

"Sound the Alarms"

Fear is the lizard's reaction to unknown territory. Therefore, when you step outside the box that once tried to contain you … you will often notice the lizard rears its silly head by climbing the walls, planting seeds of doubt about whether you can do this, or not, and has all signs pointing to getting back in the box with the lid on. That's the "safe zone," and no one can hurt you, disappoint you, or affect you there. However, what the lizard fails to tell you is that the "safe zone" is playing small, will never allow you to feel fulfilled, to experience the joy, happiness, or the lifestyle I know you desire.

How do I know? The box tried to contain me, and I busted my arse hustling in a corporate-America job for years ... to only find myself discouraged, stuck, limited in my capabilities to grow, shift, and evolve.... Limited in my financial abundance, limited in the freedom, a concrete prison schedule that not even Al Capone could chisel his way through. How did it feel? Two words. Twelve letters. *Like shitakes*. It felt horrible, it made me feel unworthy, less than, like this was the end of the road, miserable, and fluff is this all I'm capable of?

One day, I put on a set of pretty-girl bawz, and said fluff it. I walked into work, checked in with my intuition, and asked if it was in alignment with my highest self ... the answer of course was heck yeah. Keep in mind, I did not have a plan B of any sort. All I had was my trust, belief, and faith that the Universe had my back. Well, that day, I resigned from my corporate (middle-fingers in the air) position and took two weeks paid vacation as my two-week's notice. Yep, sure as heck did. Best fluffing decision I ever made because it allowed me to be the beautiful light, and bad-arse coach I am today for you.

Walked out, and my lizard was going ape shitake nuts. Promise, climbing the wall, scaling the ceiling, really fluffing bonkers. I even started hyperventilating at one point. However, after I became aware it wasn't my true thoughts, but those of my subconscious mind... I cooled my jets and enjoyed the rest of my day. I actually quit my job and fluffing celebrated at Chucky Cheese with my kids. Yep, sure did. As a coach, and an entrepreneur, I have heard every excuse in the book. Well, I need my job as I have to pay bills, I have to have money to live, I am the bread winner, and blah, blah, blah. But the truth is that fear is keeping you small and in the box. Fear is standing in your way of greatness. Fear is stopping you from what you desire. Now tell me is it true? I bet you're nodding.

Yes, it's true you must manifest some form of income to keep the roof over your head, the food in your stomach, and the electricity on... but what's not true is that you need this particular position in corporate America to do just that. Thus, after celebrating, I decided it was time to think outside the box and figure out what the fluff I desired to do. I started with a beautifully guided meditation that allowed me to clear my mind, to meet my spirit guide, and ask his arse a shift ton of questions. Well, he clearly stated that I have always known. Yep that was true, and that I've always been gifted, also true because, guess what, I was always the too-sensitive child, the grow-up, get-thick-skin, stop-imagining-things, and horribly-terrible- nightmares child. I was always the dreamer, the adventurer, and the one to leap.

Thus, so far, my handy-dandy guide was two for zero, and still hadn't answered my burning question ... what is my divine purpose? Instead he smiled and said show up and find out. You'll know. Magically the meditation came to a close, and I left more confused than I started. Well guess what happened next ... I got an inbox to go live. *Live*? What the fluff never ever never ever ... *never*... would I ever go live, I hated public speaking even though I got an A, I disliked being on center stage, even though there was something interesting about it.... Fear ... fear.... Fear....

Well, the day came to do live webcasts, and I said I am either going to faint, regurgitate, or both. I surrendered, hands in the air, took the leap of faith "all in bawz deep on me," and *boom* – instantly, the next day I had clients asking to work with me, I had messages coming left and right. I couldn't believe it. Just leap and you will know. It's the dang truth, when you surrender, everything happens, and the best part is the feeling afterward. The feeling of really showing up "all in," being of service as your highest self with the purest intentions. The moral of the story, lovelies, is feel the fear, but don't let it paralyze you. Rise above it – even if you are going to pass out, regurgitate, cuddling in a corner rocking for thirty minutes afterward – show up for yourself. Show up for those who need to hear your beautiful message and trust me, you will indeed be rewarded.

Don't let fear put you in a state of stuck, paralysis, or keep you in a dang glass box that you don't belong in. I have learned that all fear is of course is ego ... but it's also when you really want something to be. Fear arises, because holy shitake what if you lose someone you love by being successful, what if no one likes you, what if you hear crickets, what if your grandma sees you drop the f-bomb? All of these irrational, untrue questions will flood the gates ... if you allow them. What you can do instead is tap, tappity, tap, meditate, listen to music, sound healing, yoga, reiki, or even paint.

One amazing visualization tool I teach to all of my clients when they are first awakening or becoming more aware of their beautiful subconscious lizard is picturing a boom box. Yep. That eighties version of a sound machine, and I want you to see that extra-large volume knob and see yourself turning it down from ten to two. As you do this, I want you to notice that the lizard's madness is becoming less and less. It's as if he's slowly getting sleepy. Then the last thing I have them do is actually going to sound odd but I promise you, it works. I want you to stroke your forehead as though your petting your lizard, and boom, he's calm. It really does happen like that. As long as you set the intention and become aware, there are a multitude of techniques that can really help ice his arse in a beautiful way.

Another beautiful technique that I use with my clients is asking them to tell me whether what the fear says is true? (Hint: it's not.) If not, tell me three ways you know it's not true. Some responses for this scenario might be: My grandma drops the f-bomb all the time, and watches soap operas on television. No one that really loved me would leave over being more successful – if anything, they would cheer me on. Well, I am a pretty dang likeable person, so it's hard to believe no one would like me. This not only calms your lizard by letting him know "Oh we're okay," but it also confirms in your mind's eye that you are indeed perfectly, imperfectly fine. That no harm will come to you for stepping outside of the box.

Keep in mind, your belief in yourself, and trust in the Universe must be stronger than the fear of not getting what you want. Another tool you can use is to ask yourself "What is the absolute worst bloody thing that could happen by going live?" I could trip and fall on my face. Well, the truth is no one scales the Rockies without slipping a few times. Thus, the important thing is to dust yourself off, and get back on. What else could happen? Well I could stutter or become a deer in headlights.... Well, the beautiful thing about that is they may think the screen has frozen, or that you were having technical issues, and if you really want to have some fun just make some hilarious facial expressions or do the Mr. Bean walk down pretend stairs. I mean honestly, the worst that could happen is that you make several people laugh today. Well heck isn't that amazing? That you get to spread joy, and love? Hmm ... kind of sounds like a beautiful mission to me.

The real question is "How badly you want it?" If you want success, abundance, wealth, love, or whatever the heck else you dream up ... then you will find a way to make it happen. Why? Because that's what we do. The greatest gift that we have is our magnificent mind. You can't just say, "Well, I want it..." well, that's not going to get you anywhere. You need to be "all in," and taking action because taking action is how you show the Universe you want it, and it's also how you get excited about making shitakes happen. Keep in mind, it's super important to differentiate between what you desire, and what you should do. Fluff should... should shouldn't be a word. There I said it. Really and truly, should is someone else's ideas, opinions, and game plans for us. It's not our own. Therefore, leave should out of the mix altogether.

Remember, that fear is indecisiveness and that is how you get stuck. Remaining right where you are for as long as you allow the lizard to be in control of your most precious gift, "your mind." Thus, you need to remember that there are no wrong choices, only lessons, and they come with the territory anyway. Therefore, it's super-duper important that you realize making a decision is freedom, it's shackles off, and often turns right on into what your next step is. Therefore, just make a choice already. Hint: always bet on yourself. You are worth the risk and trust me, you'll see that when you are putting yourself first and being of service, you'll never fail.

Another extremely important tip I want to make you super aware of is making sure that once you have made your decision whether "yay, or nay" you want to stop yourself from negotiating. Thus, decide whether you are either all in, or you pass entirely. Keeping the decision-making process in the black-and-white spectrum will only assure your success, especially in the beginning. Once you allow yourself to negotiate, to barter, or trade, you will start to notice your ability to procrastinate, to make excuses, and to not follow-through show up. Thus, what usually happens to clients is they start out in what I will refer to as the honeymoon phase, loving life, full of excitement at the newness, and then bam... they decide well I can do it tomorrow, I have until next week, and it never gets done ... or it's so dang rushed that they are pulling their hair out to get it completed. Trust me, I have been there more than once, and it's not a great place to be. It's filled to the brim with overwhelm, anxiety, stress, and the lizard is climbing the walls. Therefore, just avoid the grey area, and you will cut out that indecisive aspect altogether because the number one area most clients state that is an issue on their behalf is not following through with the promises they made to themselves, as well as the promises they made to others. For example, I had a client just last week that told me she invested in a six-thousand-dollar program, and got bored after the first two weeks, so she just stopped showing up, let it go, disappeared, and was never to be heard of again. Of course, I helped her chalk that up to a very expensive lesson. The fact is, you have to shift or get off the pot – so a wise mentor once told me – and it's truer than true.

Chapter Ten

CREATING A LINE IN THE SAND

"I can and I will. Don't believe me – just watch."
– Bruno Mars

"Did Someone Order Boundaries?"

Creating lines in the sand is all about boundaries. Yep, super-duper important lesson because without boundaries, you are likely to get burnt-out, frustrated, bitter, angry, and just fed the fluff up. Therefore, boundaries serve a very important purpose to keep you from not only over-giving, but to keep your clients from setting unrealistic expectations. For example, I have this client named Sally, and she constantly calls me all hours of the night, texts me all hours of the day, and expects a quicker than shitakes response. This unrealistic expectation was created due to a lack of … yep you guessed it: Boundaries. As a coach, it's on me to create the line in the sand. Therefore, by failing to do so, I allowed this beautiful behavior to show up. Thus, Sally was only doing what anyone without boundaries would, reaching out for help. Remember, ask and you shall receive. It's quite beautiful once you are able to see the truth and own your shitakes.

Well how in the heck do you fix it? Simple. All you have to do is arrange a chitty-chat, tea chat with Sally, and explain that now that business is really starting to boom you are having to start instilling boundaries around the hours you'll be readily available. Therefore, your new availability is _____ Monday through Friday, and you will respond to any private messages, or text messages within 24-48 business hours. (This is fair). If Sally says well what if I need your help and it's Saturday at 2 a.m., and I cannot reach you? You kindly smile, and say Sally I totally understand, change is always scary, and trust me ... I'm the first to admit it, but honestly how likely is it that you will need me so badly at 2 a.m. on a Saturday that couldn't wait till the morning hours? She of course would sigh, and say, "You know you're right. I guess my lizard was popping up there." Yes indeed, it was. This is one beautiful way of implementing boundaries.

Another clever way of setting boundaries is by placing hours of operation on your social media profiles, on your client contracts, on your website, as well as the best means of contacting you during and after office hours. You can also clearly state that you will respond within 24-48 business hours unless it is an emergency, then your discretion will be used. This is another way of drawing your line in the sand without having to tip-toe around the tulips.

The hardest boundaries to create are the ones with family, and that's what we are going to discuss next. I know you've probably had family, friends, kids, dogs, uncles, moms, brothers, sisters, grandparents who have stepped over the line, or tread right past the invisible boundaries you've set in the past. How did it feel? Like shitakes, right? Truthfully, it probably frustrated, irritated, and upset the fluff out of you because we assume they are family – they should know better. Funny thing is… family usually is the last to know, especially when it comes to boundaries. They often feel they have relaxed or special privileges because you are part of their A-team. However, the truth is, if you feel strongly about the particular boundaries you have in place and want family members to abide by the rules … then you will have to communicate effectively as such. For example, "Joe, I know I agreed to let you stay at the house for a few nights, but this afternoon … I didn't realize I was going to come home to dirty clothing and cheeseburger wrappers being left all over the floor. I don't mind you staying with me, I actually quite enjoy it … as it's not so lonely, but we have to have some ground rules. One, as an adult please make sure to pick up after yourself, as you know I work full-time hours and just cannot come home to that." (Hint: This is a very made-up scenario, but you get the gist.)

Chapter Eleven

FACE THE WOMAN IN THE MIRROR

"The flower doesn't dream of the bee.
It blossoms and the bee comes."

– Mark Nepo

"Smexy and I Know It"

"If you want to make the world a better place, take a look in the mirror, and make that change." – Michael Jackson. Truth be told, if you crave a different outcome, and find yourself tired of running face first into the same fluffin' wall ... Then it's time you consider a change.

Remember, what got you here won't get you where you desire to be. Therefore, you have to make a decision to be "all in" on you, and live life in the present moment, on the edge of your seat. You have a calling, a purpose, and message to share with the world. They are waiting for you to face the woman in the mirror and show up. That being said, this chapter is all about taking a deep, long look in to the mirror, and not only accepting what you see, but learning to love the shitakes out of yourself. Thus, this is where you embrace your physical self, the hub, the taxi, the smexy skinsuit, in which you walk upon this Earth.

Keep in mind, this is often the last straw, and one of the most difficult because we are not kind to ourselves. We often find ourselves comparing our body to spray-tanned, photo-shopped models in magazines. Which leaves us feeling less than extraordinary. We often feel shame, guilt, and disappointment around our own body because it's not perfect. However, what body is? (Exactly.) What we fail to realize is that we chose the body we currently reside in, and there's always a reason. Trust, believe, and know you are perfectly imperfect in your own dang right.

In order to show up as your highest, most confident self, you have to be confident about what you see in the mirror. If you go on a livecast, a Zoom conference, or a video series not feeling comfortable in your own skinsuit ... you may forget your topic, freeze up, or even forego the whole dang kit-and-caboodle. Most of the time it's option three. You'll find yourself doing everything possible to skip it, cancel it, and I have witnessed hosts actually not show up. Why? Because their lizard reared its silly head, and planted seeds of doubt ... the next thing you know they are on a downward spiral, experiencing overwhelm. This brings you back to awareness, and turning around thoughts before they can take on a life of their own. Also, you are seeing that holy shift fear can make or break your personal as well as your professional life. If you allow fear to take over, you'll be in auto-pilot, and you may be at a standstill, or experiencing income-cap issues.

The first exercise you can do to get comfortable with who you currently are, is often referred to as "mirror work." Mirror work is a sure way to learn to love the shitakes out of yourself and see the world as a safe and loving place. In order to do mirror work effectively, I teach my clients that first let's uncover some issues you have with yourself. For example, my thighs look like KFC's crispy chicken. My arms look like they have batwings. My arse is too flat, my nose is too big, or maybe you simply hate your smile. Whatever the issue, or area of least satisfaction with yourself, I want you to create the list. While doing this, you are going to notice emotions start stirring around. Don't be surprised if you feel a tug at your heart strings, a discomfort in your gut, or you may even start crying snotty booger tears. Allow yourself to feel the feels ... this is an essential part of the whole dang process: Admitting to yourself how you really feel about you.

The next step is where we turn this bull crap around. Therefore, we start by selecting a few positive affirmations. Which – remember from earlier – are truly messages directed at your subconscious (a.k.a. the "lizard") in order to cool his jets, and to plant seeds of healing for your developing self-confidence, and self-esteem, and which will create a space of inner peace. Thus, affirmations are simply methods of self-talk, and as you all know, this shitake works.

Here is a list of affirmations to get you started:
- I am worthy.
- I am enough.
- I am confident.
- I am beautiful.
- I am worthy of love.
- I am love, and I love who I am.
- I am a beautiful being, and I am full of joy.
- I am perfectly imperfect in every single way.

Now, the key to putting these wheels in motion, is to repeat these beautiful phrases or mantras while looking into the mirror. It's quite powerful. Why? Because the mirror reflects the feelings you have about yourself back to yourself. It opens your eyes, and you become immediately aware of where you are resisting and where you are open and flowing. Thus, it clearly shows you what thoughts you will need to change if you want to accept where you are, who you are, love the shitakes out of yourself, and live a blissfully fulfilling life.

Keep in mind, mirror work is going to not only help you change your perspective, but make you so much more aware, and as you all know, awareness is key. Also, the big factor in any tool or process you are learning here today is practice. Practice implementing the process. You have to be consistent because that is the only way to change patterns you have had for thirty-plus years, and it's the only way to break vicious cycles of chasing your tail. Keep in mind, as you continue repeating the exercise you will start to notice a shift – a gradual shift – in how you view yourself, how you carry yourself, and the way that you think.

Not only will your posture improve, but now you notice you don't dislike your nose, you actually might even like it. Which is a *huge* deal. Not only does it boost your self-confidence, self-esteem, and self-love, but it actually allows you to get comfortable in front of yourself. In front of a pretend, if you will, camera. Keep in mind, that most of the time when you do a livecast it is indeed reflecting your image. Thus, this would only ease your anxiety, and allow you to step forward.

The next exercise I want to discuss with you is what I like to refer to as "Body Talk." This is when you use positive affirmations, phrases, or compliments about your own beautiful body. For example, "I am sexy. I am powerful. I am confident. I am loved. I am adored. I am worthy. I am enough. I am limitless. I am beautiful. I am everything that I dream of. I am successful. I am creative. I am lovable. I am amazeballs." These are just a few body-confidence affirmations you can recite or use daily to boost not only the distorted version you see of yourself, but to also allow you to gain confidence in yourself, what you have to offer, and how you show up for the world.

There will always be bumps in the road. That is just part of the process. We are always growing, expanding, shifting, and spreading our wings. Therefore, we are bound to hit a bump or two. The important thing is that when you fall, you pick yourself up, brush yourself off, and try again.

When you face a hurdle, it's important to do some deep breathing, inhaling in through your nose, and exhaling all the stress, overwhelm, and madness out through your mouth. I would do this three times, and then allow yourself to fully focus on what is blocking you from where you desire to be. Is it worth it? If not, tell me three ways you know for sure without a phantom of a doubt that make these statements untrue.

Chapter Twelve

CHALLENGES

"But you know, happiness can be found even in the darkest of times, if only one remembers to turn on the light"

– J.K Rowling

"Cue the Lights"

Now that you have all of the keys to the castle ... it's important for you to realize that shitake is still going to come up. Yep! Keep in mind, this book is not a fairy-tale (even though it is quite a bit magical). It is more of a love story to successful making shitakes happen in your own life.

Therefore, it's important to realize that even though you have all of the beautiful tools to add to your bag ... you may still face the occasional lizard climbing the walls, freaking the fluff out, and spiraling downward into the abyss. Yep. It happens to everyone, whether they discuss it or not.

Thus, obstacles arise, and we are always confronted with a decision on whether to leap, or to retreat. It's that fight or flight that we discussed earlier in the book. The decision process is always yours, and because of the beautiful free will you have ... therefore, the actual outcome is all on you. Will you rise or will you tuck your tail between your legs, and run in the face of animosity?

This decision is yours to make ... this book, as amazing as it is, cannot do it for you, and therefore, cannot be responsible for the outcome. What I mean is the tools shared with you throughout the course of the book are to help you on making these beautifully diverse decisions, as well as to give you steps to take in order to become more aware of when that lizard is rearing its head. As you know the lizard, and what is often referred to as resistance "pulling back," is sneaky, and can stop you right in your tracks. Thus, it deters that magical train filled to the brim with what you desire off the route the Universe put in place for you. Thus, it's super-duper important that you are always checking in, using your intuition, and awareness to pinpoint any signs of a possible derailment before it actually happens.

You've also been given the tools necessary to turn the lizard down from ten to two on the volume control, or to tap, tappity, tap him back into the cave he came out of. You have learned as well as the importance of checking in with your gut to make sure that any decision is in the highest alignment with yourself. You have learned the importance of feeling the fear and doing it anyways, as well as how to show up, and make shitakes happen. You have learned strategies and exercises that, if followed, are able to lead you to what you desire the most. However, the key to all of these beautiful pieces is you. Your intention, your willingness to do the work, and how you choose to show up for yourself.

Thus, keep in mind that sometimes it may feel like you are dropping pieces, that people are falling out of your life, and opportunities are shrinking. Let me just say, this is absolutely normal, and the Universe's way of aligning everything for you. Remember, in order to make room for what we desire ... we have to shed the shitakes that no longer are aligned or serve our highest good. This would include people, opportunities, physical, emotional, and mental baggage. While this can be a difficult space to be in, know that it is all part of the greater scheme of things, the bigger process, and it is only temporary.

One beautiful exercise that I have found to help clients, as well as myself when the lizard tries to rear his lovely little head is what I call the "gratitude jar." This is when you take a mason jar, a soup jar, a bucket, a container with a lid, and you can put a slit in the top or you can just screw and unscrew it ... it's totally whatever feels right for you. Then you want to beautify the jar. Make it more aesthetically attractive to you and put it in plain view for you to see. Every single day, you're going to want to add two or three slips of paper for anything you are grateful for throughout the day. For example, I am grateful for eight hours of sleep. I am grateful for the air in my lungs, and the sun in the sky. I am grateful for the $20 bill I found in my pocket, etc.

The key to this exercise is to feel gratitude daily, and I always state to do the jar until it's full or for thirty days, and after thirty days, open the jar, and read back over all of the slips you have placed in the jar. This will make you feel uber-grateful, you may even be overcome with emotion, and it will indeed help you maintain your high-vibe. Now keep in mind, another trick to this exercise is, anytime you feel low vibe, like your shifting, or having a challenging day ... you can open the gratitude jar and read through a few slips in order to raise your vibration.

Promise, the tools you have acquired in this book really do work once put into action, and once you give up the resistance. Let's talk about another beautiful client of mine, Rebecca. Rebecca definitely had trouble switching auto-pilot off because she worried about everyone else but herself. She cared if Becky from the cafeteria was eating healthy, she cared if the school bus driver got enough sleep (for more than one reason). She cared if the mailman had enough water, so that he did not dehydrate, but what Rebecca did not ever think about was how she felt, what she needed, and this was definitely one of her biggest obstacles. Thus, after completing the exercises from the "shed the shitakes" list, the desire list, the vision board, the affirmations, mirror work ... she was living in joy, making shitakes happen, but she every time she tweaked something in her routine or it didn't go the way that she felt it should ... her lizard came out, and acted as though the world was ending and it was all going to implode. Thus, through revisiting the beautiful exercises, the meditations, the tappity, tap, tapping, and becoming more aware, she was able to turn everything around much faster than the time before. However, what really helped Rebecca overcome this lizard challenge was implementing the "gratitude jar." This would always perk her up within seconds because to see what she really had going in her favor, and how many people loved, supported, and lifted her up ... even if it was perfect strangers, to start to realize the difference she was making in the world by just smiling at Suzie the neighbor ... it felt amazing, and instantly kicked off the auto-pilot switch, so that she could keep stepping further away from the confinements of that box, and living her life for her.

Keep in mind, change is uncomfortable, scary as fluff, and will challenge the very core of your trust and belief system. Therefore, don't cave, don't pull back, and sure as heck, don't stop. Change is a beautiful thing because it's what's necessary to get you right where you desire to be, and with change come challenges. They work hand-in-hand because your body, your lizard wants to resist.... We don't like change – it's unsafe, uncertain, and you can't fully see the road ahead, and the outcome is unknown, but the beautiful thing is, if you have fully surrendered to the process, you don't need to see ahead. If you let go of control, and surrender to your trust, believe in yourself, as well as the Universe, then you will see this is only a temporary situation for long-term gain. What is the gain you ask? It's what you seek the most. Remember, the more we desire it, the more adverse the challenge will be. Because our confidence, our faith, our trust – it's all tested to see are we truly ready.

Are we open to receiving the gifts the Universe has in store? Again, the decision is all yours, and the question is "Are you all in bawz deep on yourself, your dreams, or will you run at the first sight of adversity?'

You are indeed here for such a bigger purpose, and you have a beautiful message to share with the world. Therefore, when you heal yourself, invest in yourself, be all in on you ... you are also healing the world. Yep. That's how it works. As you grow, shift, and change ... by showing up as your highest self, you also are of service in a higher, more meaningful, impactful beautiful way which then heals the world. Even if it's just feeling confident enough to carry on a conversation with someone at the grocery store behind you. Don't see the insignificance in the interaction, but the beauty. What if that was the only conversation with another being she has had in a long time, what if that made her day, and shifted a deep-seeded something within her... a belief that human beings no longer care about one another? What if your smile actually helped lift her spirits because she had a horrible day? Aren't these all magical outcomes in their own right? Are any one of them less worthy of praise, of the validation that you are indeed making a difference? Doesn't it feel good to know how fluffing far you've come? How amazing you truly are, and what one seemingly simple act of kindness as your highest self can do for so many? Pretty amazing right? Guess what my dear, this is just the beginning. Which is why it's so important to see the glass half full. See the bigger picture, see past your nose, and know that you are indeed meant for greater things.

CONCLUSION

"There are far better things ahead than
any we leave behind."

– C.S. Lewis

"No Turning Back Now"

You've finally reached the point of no return. There is no going back, as you are starting to really see the possibility. You are starting to shift, to change, to grow and expand. You are starting to see that not everything is against you, and that the Universe does indeed have your back. You are going through a beautiful transformation, a metamorphosis if you will, from the caterpillar to the beautiful butterfly. Keep in mind, you may still have wobbly legs, but you can still soar. You are indeed called to be of service as your highest light, and many are awaiting the sharing of your beautiful message.

Unfortunately, this doesn't mean you won't struggle, or face challenging hurdles along the way... this journey is all about the road ahead which is never a linear line, but more of an up and down (ebb and flow style). Thus, there will be absolutely beautiful moments where you see yourself as this beautiful light, radiating from the heart-center, illuminating the world, and feeling like a magical fluffing unicorn.... Then there will be times when you feel like you got hit by a Mack truck, and that is absolutely normal. However, from this book you have learned a variety of tools that you can implement in order to fall forward. Falling forward is knowing that this shift, this uncomfortable feeling is temporary, and the most beautiful secret about shifting is that after the clouds part ... you get to see the sun. Yep! You get to bask in its radiant glow, and really feel like you're on cloud nine.

Trust me, I always welcome the shift because it only means you're growing, learning, shifting, and evolving. Isn't that what we are here for? Keep in mind, this is just the tip of the iceberg, so get excited as there is so much more, and you are so dang ready. Therefore, it's time to put on your beautiful warrior suit, and if you haven't yet ... it's time to take the flying leap outside your comfort zone. Remember, what got you here, won't get you there.

Thus, it's time to put your pretty bawz on, and rise up, like the phoenix. Trust, believe, and know that you are indeed here with a very important message to share with the world. The world needs you, and yes, you can absolutely implement all of these steps on your own, but how long have you tried that route? How has it served you so far, and lastly are you tired of running face first into the same fluffing wall?

If you are nodding or saying yes then here's the deal. It's so much easier, more efficient to have a tour guide to hold your hand and illuminate the way. Together, we will create a customized plan of action just for you because as you know from reading this book … I don't believe in the one-size-fits-all approach, and love to tailor the solution to your exact needs. Keep in mind, with my guidance, we will arrive at our destination in quantum-leaping fashion. With me, everything will come together with ease and flow, and not only will you have the world's greatest cheerleader … but you'll have an accountability partner that is willing to gently put a foot in your arse if need be.

If you are ready to show up and make a difference not only in your own personal and professional life, but the lives of so many others, then this is the plan for you. Together we make quite the powerhouse team, and a dang force to be reckoned with. If you are all-in committed to your movement, your growth, yourself, and willing to do the soul work to get you where you desire to be, then you will absolutely notice the expedited rate in which shitake starts to happen, and manifest into your life with the ease and flow of a bad-arse coach.

FURTHER READING

You Are a BadAss at Making Money by Jen Sincero

The Secret by Rhonda Byrne

The Subtle Art of Not Giving A F*** by Mark Manson

Harry Potter by J.K. Rowling

The Universe Has Your Back by Gabby Bernstein

The Difference by Dr. Angela Lauria

White Hot Truth by Danielle LaPorte

Unf*ck Yourself by Gary John Bishop

ACKNOWLEDGMENTS

Thank you to my pretty amazing husband who has supported my journey whole-heartedly, and allowed me to continue to grow, shift, change, and spread my wings. Even doing some of the woo-wooest of stuff. I love you with all of my heart, and I am so grateful every single day for the life we have created.

Thank you to my two beautiful children, Maggie Lou and Christopher Michael. They have been my most precious blessings, a divine gift that I cherish, learn, and grow with every single day. I love the play, the youth they bring into my life, and the adventures we share. I cannot wait to see where the yellow brick road leads us all.

Thank you to my amazing mother- and father-in-law who have believed in me from the very beginning before I ever truly believed in myself. Who knew that the possibilities were limitless, and that my past could never define my future. Thank you for showing me parental love I never had. Thank you for being patient with me while I processed and allowing me to blossom before your very eyes. Also, thank you for being such amazing parents, grand-parents, and all-around amazing people. I am forever grateful.

Thank you to Dr. Angela Lauria and the Difference Press for seeing in me something I didn't quite fully see in myself.

I submitted my application on a whim because I have always felt called to write. I have always loved writing, even with my unique language. I remember the moment I heard back from Norman that I was in, and that I was inspiring. I about fell out of my chair. I never even fully realized that this was possible. What a dream come true, and a beautiful journey it has been. Thank you for believing in me, and so many others. It's a beautiful gift you share with the world.

I also want to thank the Universe for being patient with my sacred rebel self and allowing me to share my beautiful messages with the world. Thank you for always having my back, and for allowing me to shift, grow, love unconditionally even in the hardest of times ... Thank you, thank you, thank you. I know this is only the beginning.

ABOUT THE AUTHOR

Christie Hayden is an intuitive healer, mindset visionary, and bad-arse business coach who has helped countless women transform their personal and professional lives via her coaching, masterminds, group programs, public speaking gigs, newsletters, and through her amazing new book. Her purpose in life is to help raise the vibration of the world through unconditional love and positivity, by helping women whom are struggling to find their place in this world... who may be facing obstacles, feeling overwhelmed, stuck, or like they just have bad fluffin' luck... reach a higher vibration, and overcome whatever is holding them back from the life they truly desire. She helps women find their voice in this sometimes-chaotic world, and lift, support, and love themselves, as well as creates a strategy to help them live the life they truly desire. If you would like to learn more about Christie and her work, you can join her below.

Website: https://christie-hayden.mykajabi.com
Email: ChristieMHayden@gmail.com
Facebook: https://www.facebook.com/mindsetchristie
Instagram: https://www.instagram.com/mindsetchristie

ABOUT DIFFERENCE PRESS

Difference Press offers entrepreneurs, including life coaches, healers, consultants, and community leaders, a comprehensive solution to get their books written, published, and promoted. A boutique-style alternative to self-publishing, Difference Press boasts a fair and easy-to-understand profit structure, low-priced author copies, and author-friendly contract terms. Its founder, Dr. Angela Lauria, has been bringing to life the literary ventures of hundreds of authors-in-transformation since 1994.

LET'S MAKE A DIFFERENCE WITH YOUR BOOK

You've seen other people make a difference with a book. Now it's your turn. If you are ready to stop watching and start taking massive action, reach out.

"Yes, I'm ready!"

In a market where hundreds of thousands books are published every year and are never heard from again, all participants of The Author Incubator have bestsellers that are actively changing lives and making a difference.

"In two years we've created over 250 bestselling books in a row, 90% from first-time authors." We do this by selecting the highest quality and highest potential applicants for our future programs.

Our program doesn't just teach you how to write a book—our team of coaches, developmental editors, copy editors, art directors, and marketing experts incubate you from book idea to published bestseller, ensuring that the book you create can actually make a difference in the world. Then we give you the training you need to use your book to make the difference you want to make in the world, or to create a business out of serving your readers. If you have life-or world-changing ideas or services, a servant's heart, and the willingness to do what it REALLY takes to make a difference in the world with your book, go to http://theauthorincubator.com/apply/ to complete an application for the program today.

OTHER BOOKS BY DIFFERENCE PRESS

Your Key to the Akashic Records: Fulfill Your Soul's Highest Potential

by Jiayuh Chyan

...But I'm Not Racist!: Tools for Well-Meaning Whites

by Kathy Obear

Who the Fuck Am I To Be a Coach: A Warrior's Guide to Building a Wildly Successful Coaching Business From the Inside Out

by Megan Jo Wilson

A Graceful Goodvye: A New Outlook on Death

by Susan B. Mercer

Lasting Love At Last: The Gay Guide To Attracting the Relationship of Your Dreams

by Amari Ice

Finding Time to Lead: Seven Practices to Unleash Outrageous Potential

by Leslie Peters

The Magical Business Method: Define Your Stardust, Attract Your Tribe, Make Lots of Money

by Tamara Arnold

THANK YOU

As a thank you, for purchasing a copy of my book, and to help you take action, I'm offering you a one-time free gift to help you "make the shitakes" happen with a brand-spankin' new webinar I've created just for you.

Thus, if you are tired of feeling like life is happening to you instead of for you? Tired of chasing your fluffin' tail, and never getting shitake accomplished? What if I told you that life doesn't have to be hard, and that there is indeed an easier way?

Ready to be all-in, bawz-deep in on you?

You can sign up now at: https://christie-hayden.mykajabi.com/freegift

I look forward to seeing your beautiful self soon!

-xx
Christie

Printed in Great Britain
by Amazon